Simply Jiggy

THE ASHOKA COOK SCHOOL COOKBOOK

Simply Jiggy

THE ASHOKA COOK SCHOOL COOKBOOK

Jiggy Majhu

Photography by Alan Donaldson

First published 2012

by Black & White Publishing Ltd

29 Ocean Drive, Edinburgh EH6 6JL

1 3 5 7 9 10 8 6 4 2   12 13 14 15

ISBN: 978 1 84502 495 6

The book is available online at www.ashokashop.com
registered office 23 Crow Road, Glasgow G11 7RT Tel. 0141 342 5200

A CIP catalogue record for this book is available from the British Library.

Book designed by Creative Link, North Berwick

Printed and bound in Poland

www.hussarbooks.pl

ACKNOWLEDGEMENTS

Thanks go to

Hardial Singh (Dali) Master Chef and Genius (Ashton Lane) • Chefs Shamil (West End), Chandan (Bearsden) and Ashish (Green Chilli Café) • Chef James Tagg for his guidance (Executive Chef Man Utd) • Ketan Nahar • Naz Aksi (Ashton Lane) • Imtiaz Aslam for all his hard work • All our Partner Franchise Directors and staff of the Group • Head Office Staff • Our bosses at Bank Of Scotland for keeping us safe during the turbulent times and continuing to support our business • All our loyal Ashoka customers: we are humbled and thank you with all our hearts for your support since 1973

Thanks also go to my family

Mummy Majhu (Pavittar Majhu) • Poochi Aunty • All my nieces and nephews • Nimmi, Gin and Vin • Kidd • Craig • Lynn

I would like to thank my four wonderful boys: Anish, Nitesh, Arin and Krish for understanding my long absences away from home while developing this book. I love you with all my heart.

I would like to express my gratitude and love to my husband and soul mate Sanjay Majhu, Mr Ashoka, for his support, inspiration and encouragement throughout this book.

To book classes, buy spices or any utensils which are in this Cookbook go to:
www.ashokacookschool.com

or visit the following:

Ashoka Cook School, Phoenix Leisure Park Linwood PA1 2AB • Tel: 0141 889 4123

Head Office and Corporate Bookings, Ashoka Cookschool, 23 Crow Rd, Glasgow G11 7RT
Tel: 0141 342 5200

Other Harlequin Restaurants

Ashoka Ashton Lane	0141 337 1115	Ashoka Bearsden	0141 570 0075
Ashoka Southside	0141 637 0711	Ashoka Quay	0141 429 4492
Ashoka West End	0141 339 3371	Ashoka Livingston	01506 416 622
Ashoka Coatbridge	01236 437 181	Ashoka Dundee	01382 833 157
Green Chilli Café	0141 337 6378	Las Ramblas	0141 942 1380

www.ashokarestaurants.com

New restaurant opening at time of publishing: Ashoka Edinburgh, 97 Hanover St, EH2 1DJ

Dedicated to my mum, Kosheila Kaur

A special thanks to Dali for all his guidance, advice and
dedication in helping me develop all the recipes.

I would also like to thank Janice Greig and Christina Wilson for
all their support and help.

Jiggy x

CONTENTS

INTRODUCTION

Growing up in a big family I was always amazed at how my mum cooked for so many of us. I remember her cooking two curries during the day for lunch and then cooking another curry for the evening meal. We would eat the leftover food from lunch with the fresh curry she had just made; nothing went to waste. Everything was made fresh every day, there was no such thing as a takeaway in our house. My sisters and I would set the table for dinner, and often would help mum butter the chapatis to give them that extra softness which made our mouths water.

Another memory I have was when my sister got married and in those days there were not many outdoor caterers. My mum insisted that she would do all the food for the wedding. She got all her friends together and made everything from the samosas to the ladoo (Indian sweetmeat).

I lost my mum at a very young age but the first dish she taught me how to make was fresh yoghurt. I remember being so proud of the fact that I could make this, so every time there was yoghurt needed I would always volunteer.

Due to my mum's influence it was a natural progression for me to find my own style of cooking and now being a wife, a mother of four boys and a working mum, means I have to cook good, quick, nutritious food.

My husband and I opened our first restaurant in 1992 where he became a partner in the Spice of Life Restaurant, Argyle St, now known as the Green Chilli Café. After a turbulent eight years we finally bought out our partners in 2000 and we were quite happy running one restaurant.

But my husband does not sit idle and before too long, in 2005, he decided to buy out the whole Ashoka Group. Being honest I wasn't too happy because as usual I knew he would make me do all the work . . . I'm saying nothing . . .

I love working with Dali and all our other chefs, developing recipes for our customers, but my inspiration came from my mum. Being the wife of Glasgow's curry king, Sanjay, he would always expect the best of home cooking, so I had Glasgow's biggest critic to please. That's a job in itself.

We are blessed to be doing what we love. Ashoka is a truly family business, and my Ashoka Cook School was just a natural next step for us. So I decided we needed a cookbook which was easy to follow and would be the next step from the first Ashoka cookbook which has sold nearly 10,000 copies.

I hope you like making the recipes in this book as much as I have loved writing them.

Jiggy Majhu

BASIC COOKING ESSENTIALS

Here are recipes for some of the essential ingredients that you will use throughout this book, from ginger and garlic paste to ginger juice. Most of them can be prepared in advance and will stay fresh for some time.

CASHEW NUT PASTE

Place 50g of unsalted cashew nuts in a small bowl and pour in enough water to cover all the cashew nuts.

Leave for 30 minutes, then mix to a smooth paste in a blender. Can be stored for 2-3 days in the fridge in an airtight container.

GREEN CHILLI PASTE

Place 100g chopped green chillies and 7tbsp of vegetable oil in a blender and blend to a smooth paste.

The chilli paste will keep for 3 weeks in the fridge in an airtight container.

GINGER AND GARLIC PASTE

Place 50g garlic cloves, 50g peeled and chopped fresh ginger and 5tbsp of vegetable oil in a blender and blend to a smooth paste.

The paste will keep for 4 weeks in the fridge in an airtight container.

GARAM MASALA

4 tbsp coriander seeds (dhania)
1 tbsp cumin seeds (jeera)
1 tbsp black peppercorns
1½ tsp black cumin seeds (kala jeera)
1½ tsp ginger powder
3-4 black cardamom pods
¾ tsp cloves
2 2.5cm cinnamon sticks broken up
¾ tsp bay leaves, crushed

Put all the ingredients except the ginger powder, in a heavy-based pan on a medium heat. Gently roast until they turn a few shades darker, stirring occasionally to prevent the spices from burning.

When the spices are roasted turn off the heat and allow them to cool.

Once cooled, remove the cardamom seeds from their pods and discard the husks. Mix the seeds back in with all the other roasted spices and add the ginger powder.

Grind the spices to a fine powder in a clean dry grinder.

The garam masala will keep for several months in an airtight container stored in a cool dark place.

CHAAT MASALA

3 tbsp cumin seeds (jeera)

1 tbsp coriander seeds (dhania)

1½ tsp fennel seeds (saunf)

4 tbsp green mango powder (amchoor)

3 tbsp powdered black salt

1½ tsp freshly ground black pepper

¼ tsp asafoetida (hing)

1½ tsp ginger powder

1 tsp dried powdered mint leaves

1½ tsp carom seeds (ajwain)

Heat a heavy-based pan on a medium heat. When hot, put in the cumin, coriander and fennel seeds.

Dry roast the seeds until they become a little bit darker. Stir often while roasting, to prevent the seeds from burning.

When the seeds are roasted remove them from pan and spread them out on a plate to cool.

When cool, mix the seeds with all the other ingredients and place in a clean, dry grinder and grind them to a smooth powder.

Store the chaat masala in an airtight container in a cool, dry place. Keep separate from other spices as they will take on its aroma.

The masala will keep its flavour for 2-3 months.

DRY ROASTING SPICES

To roast whole spices, place them in a small frying pan or saucepan over a medium heat and stir and toss them around for 1-2 minutes, or until they begin to look toasted and start to jump in the pan.

Place them in an airtight container and store in a cool dry place.

If the recipe requires the spices to be ground, place them in a pestle and mortar or use an electric grinder to crush them to a powder or coarsely grind them according to the recipe instructions. This will be easier to do now that they have been roasted.

GINGER JUICE

Peel and grate several large slices of fresh ginger, squeeze out the ginger juice from the grated pieces into a small bowl.

This can be done by squeezing through a cheesecloth or garlic press.

Make the juice as required for recipes as it will only keep for 2 days in the fridge.

STARTERS

The best part of any meal is the starter. It's where you get a taste of things to come. For me the most convenient starter is a vegetable pakora because I always have the ingredients at home and it's so easy to make.

My favourite is the chilli paneer because when you taste paneer on its own it is very bland but this recipe seems to transform it as it is full of lovely flavours.

I also love making the salmon tikka and the tava machi as it's a great way to get my children to eat fish.

Enjoy my starters.

Vegetable Pakora

INGREDIENTS

oil for deep frying

½ onion, finely chopped

½ potato, finely chopped

60g spinach (palak), chopped

½ tsp crushed coriander seeds (dhania)

1 tsp cumin seeds (jeera)

1 tsp salt

1 tsp red chilli powder

1½ tsp lemon juice

1 tsp dry fenugreek leaves (methi)

1 level tbsp ginger and garlic paste

125g gram flour (besan)

4 tbsp approx. cold water

SERVES 2
(Vegetarian)

METHOD

Heat the oil in a deep fat fryer to 170C.

In a bowl, mix the onion, potato, spinach, crushed coriander, cumin seeds, salt, red chilli powder, fenugreek, ginger and garlic paste and lemon juice. Leave to stand for 10 minutes. (This is so that the juices from the onions and potatoes can be used when adding the gram flour).

Add the gram flour and gradually add the water to form a batter.

Drop one spoonful of the mixture at a time into the oil. Fry until golden brown (the pakoras should be asteroid shaped).

Serve with pakora sauce (see page 181).

Creamy Chicken Tikka (Malai Tikka)

INGREDIENTS

40g soft cheese
(eg Philadelphia)

2 tbsp double cream

1 heaped tbsp cashew nut paste

1 tsp green chilli paste

1 tsp salt

1 large egg

1 tsp ginger and garlic paste

1 tsp lemon juice

300g chicken breast, cut into approx. 6 large pieces

SERVES 2

METHOD

Pre-heat the oven to 170C.

For the marinade
Mix the cheese, double cream, cashew paste, green chilli paste and salt in a bowl.

Whisk the egg in a separate bowl then add 2 tablespoons to the cheese mixture. Mix thoroughly then place in the fridge.

For the chicken
Mix the ginger and garlic paste with the lemon juice and use it to coat the chicken. Leave to infuse for 15 minutes.

Add the chicken to the marinade and leave it in the fridge for at least 1 hour.

Cook on a tray in the oven for 20 minutes or until the chicken is cooked through, turning the chicken once.

Spicy Indian Cheese (Chilli Paneer)

INGREDIENTS

4 tbsp vegetable oil

¼ tsp cumin seeds (jeera)

¼ onion, cut into chunks

2 small green chillies, chopped

1 tsp ginger and garlic paste

¼ tsp turmeric powder (haldi)

¼ fresh tomato, finely chopped

½ tsp green chilli paste

¼ tsp salt

100g paneer, cut into cubes

1 tbsp fresh coriander for garnish

SERVES 2
(Vegetarian)

METHOD

Heat the oil in a pan, add the cumin seeds, onions and green chillies and fry until the onion becomes soft.

Add the ginger and garlic paste, turmeric, tomato, green chilli paste and salt and cook for 3 minutes.

Stir in the paneer and mix carefully so that the paneer does not break. Stir frequently for 10-15 minutes.

Garnish with the coriander and serve.

Lamb Mince Pastry (Keema Samosa)

INGREDIENTS

FOR THE FILLING
vegetable oil for deep frying

2½ tbsp vegetable oil

¼ onion, chopped

pinch cumin seeds (jeera)

½ tsp ginger and garlic paste

¼ tsp salt

¼ tsp red chilli powder

¼ tsp turmeric powder (haldi)

¼ fresh tomato

130g minced lamb

1 green chilli, chopped

1½ tbsp garden peas

pinch dried fenugreek leaves (methi), fresh coriander and garam masala

FOR THE PASTRY
Two 25cm square pieces of spring roll pastry cut into 3 equal size strips

Flour and water to make a paste

SERVES 3

METHOD

Heat the oil in deep fat fryer to 170C.

Heat the oil in a frying pan and add the onion and cumin. Fry until the onions are brown.

Add the ginger and garlic paste, salt, chilli powder and turmeric to the onion mixture and stir for one minute. Add the tomato, stir and cook for a further couple of minutes.

Add the mince and chopped green chillies and cook for 10 minutes then add the peas and cook for a further 2-3 minutes.

Add the methi, coriander and garam masala, mix well and leave to cool.

Take 2 strips of the pastry and place one on top of the other, fold one half to form a cone shape and brush underneath the cone with the paste mixture so that it sticks.

Put 4 tablespoons of the mixture in to the cone and press the mixture down gently. Fold the other half over to make a triangle and seal the outer edges with the paste, making sure the samosas are completely sealed.

Deep fry the samosas in the hot oil for 4-5 minutes until golden brown, stirring occasionally. Do not allow them to brown too quickly.

Chicken Pakora

INGREDIENTS

oil for deep frying

200g chicken breast, chopped

1 tsp lemon juice

½ tsp ginger and garlic paste

¼ tsp cumin seeds (jeera)

¼ tsp salt

¼ tsp red chilli powder

¼ tsp tikka paste

2 heaped tbsp gram flour (besan)

1 heaped tbsp self-raising flour

pinch dried fenugreek leaves (methi)

4 tbsp (approx.) water

SERVES 2

METHOD

Heat oil in a deep fat fryer to 170C.

Mix in a bowl, the lemon juice, ginger and garlic paste, cumin seeds, salt, red chilli powder and tikka paste.

Add the chicken and leave to marinate for 15 minutes.

In a separate bowl mix the gram flour, self-raising flour and a pinch of fenugreek with the water to form a batter.

Add the chicken marinade to the batter and leave to stand for a couple of minutes.

Place all the chicken in the fryer one piece at a time and fry until golden brown.

Serve with pakora sauce or a chutney (see pages 181-206).

Salmon Tikka

INGREDIENTS

1 level tsp salt

1 tsp green chilli paste

½ tsp ginger and garlic paste

½ tsp tandoori paste

1 tbsp plain yoghurt

1½ tbsp vegetable oil

¼ tsp garam masala

¼ tsp ground turmeric (haldi)

1 tbsp lemon juice

2 salmon fillets (approx 100g each)

SERVES 2

METHOD

Mix all the ingredients together in a medium-sized bowl before adding the salmon and coating it with the marinade.

Leave to marinate in the fridge for 1 hour.

Remove the salmon and place on a baking tray, covered loosely with foil. Bake in a preheated oven (160C) for approximately 17 minutes turning half way through the cooking time.

Onion Bhaji

INGREDIENTS

oil for deep frying

1 large onion, sliced

1 tsp cumin seeds (jeera)

½ tsp red chilli powder

1 tbsp lemon juice

1 level tsp salt

1 tbsp dried fenugreek leaves (methi)

½ tsp ginger and garlic paste

1 tbsp fresh coriander, chopped

5½ tbsp gram flour (besan)

3 tbsp approx. water

SERVES 4
(Vegetarian)

METHOD

Heat the oil in a deep fat fryer to 170C.

In a bowl, mix the onion, cumin seeds, salt, red chilli powder, fenugreek, lemon juice, coriander and the ginger and garlic paste. Leave to marinate for 10 minutes. (This is so that the juices from the onions can be added to the gram flour).

Add the gram flour and gradually add water. Mix all the ingredients together and shape into 4 even-sized balls.

Deep fry for 3-4 minutes. Remove the bhajis and flatten them into patties. Let the oil heat up again and refry until crispy and golden.

Serve with pakora sauce (see page 181).

King Prawns with Pickle (Achari King Prawn)

INGREDIENTS

1 level tsp salt

½ tsp turmeric powder (haldi)

1 tsp ginger and garlic paste

1 tbsp lemon juice

1 level tbsp plain yoghurt

¼ tsp garam masala

½ tsp tandoori paste

1 tsp green chilli paste

½ tsp mixed pickle blended

1 tbsp mustard oil

pinch carom seeds (ajwain)

270g king prawns shelled and de-veined

SERVES 2

METHOD

Preheat the oven to 170C.

Put all the ingredients (except the prawns) into a bowl and mix thoroughly. Add the prawns and leave to marinade in the fridge for at least 20 minutes.

Place the prawns on a baking tray and brush over any remaining marinade and cook in the oven for about 10 minutes or until ready. Be careful not to overcook the prawns or they will quickly become tough and rubbery.

Lamb Mince Kebab (Keema Kebab)

INGREDIENTS

¼ onion, finely chopped

1 tsp ginger and garlic paste

1½ tsp cumin seeds (jeera)

1 tsp red chilli powder

½ tsp garam masala

¾ tsp salt

2 green chillies

1 tbsp fresh coriander, chopped

300g lamb mince

SERVES 2

METHOD

Put the onion, ginger and garlic paste, cumin seeds, red chilli powder, garam masala, salt and green chillies into a blender and blend to a paste.

Put the mince in a bowl with all the blended ingredients and the coriander leaves and mix thoroughly.

Leave the mixture to rest for 10 minutes.

Divide the mixture into 4 equal portions, moisten hands with cold water and mould into long sausage shapes.

Place the kebabs on a baking tray in a preheated oven at 180C until cooked through.

Potato Cake (Aloo Tikki)

INGREDIENTS

2 medium potatoes, peeled and chopped

¼ tsp salt

½ tsp red chilli powder

¼ tsp cumin seeds (jeera)

1 tsp breadcrumbs

1 tsp fresh coriander, chopped

¼ tsp crushed coriander seeds (dhania)

1 level tbsp garam masala

pinch dried fenugreek leaves (methi)

vegetable oil for frying

SERVES 2
(Vegetarian)

METHOD

Boil the potatoes and mash them in a bowl. Allow them to cool down.

Add all of the other ingredients except the fenugreek and oil and mix evenly through the potato. When all the ingredients are mixed add the pinch of fenugreek and mix again.

Form the potato mixture into 4 round balls and flatten each one to make a patty.

Heat the oil in a frying pan and fry the patties gently, turning frequently until browned on both sides.

Sabzi Pakora

INGREDIENTS

¼ onion, finely chopped

¼ potato, finely chopped

handful spinach (palak)

2 tbsp chopped aubergine

1 small cauliflower floret, chopped

2 tbsp peas

1 tbsp fresh coriander, chopped

½ tsp salt

1 tsp red chilli powder

1 tsp ground coriander (dhania)

1½ tsp lemon juice

1 level tbsp ginger and garlic paste

100g gram flour (besan)

3 tbsp approx. cold water

SERVES 4
(Vegetarian)

METHOD

Heat oil in a deep fat fryer to 170C.

Mix all the ingredients together in a large bowl (except the gram flour and water). Set aside and leave to stand for 10 minutes.

Put the gram flour in the bowl with the other ingredients and add the cold water a little at a time and mix to form a smooth batter.

Drop one tablespoon of batter mix at a time into the hot oil. Continue until all the batter has been used. (Oil is at the correct temperature if after a minute the pakoras rise to the top of the oil).

Stir occasionally while the pakoras are frying. Each batch should take about 5 minutes.

Amritsari Fish

INGREDIENTS

1½ tsp ginger and garlic paste

1 tsp green chilli paste

¼ tsp mint sauce

¼ tsp chaat masala

½ tsp salt

¼ tsp black cumin seeds (kala jeera)

½ tsp dried fenugreek leaves (methi)

2 pinches fresh coriander, chopped

1½ tsp lemon juice

270g haddock, cut into 4 pieces

2 tbsp cornflour

oil to brush the griddle (tava)

SERVES 1

METHOD

Place all the ingredients in a bowl except the haddock and mix. Add the fish and coat it with the mixture.

Leave to marinade for 30 minutes.

Put the cornflour on a plate and dip each piece of fish to coat evenly on both sides.

Brush the tava with the oil and wait for it to heat up. Place the fish on the tava and cook on a medium heat for approximately 2 minutes then turn it over and cook for a further 2 minutes, turn again until the fish is cooked thoroughly.

Chicken Chaat

INGREDIENTS

300g chicken wings (4 pieces)

½ tsp salt

¼ tsp red chilli powder

½ tsp tandoori paste

1 tsp ginger and garlic paste

1½ tbsp plain yoghurt

2 tbsp vegetable oil

1 tsp lemon juice

¼ tsp turmeric powder (haldi)

¼ tsp garam masala

SERVES 2

METHOD

Place the chicken in a bowl. Add the salt, red chilli powder, tandoori paste, ginger and garlic paste, yoghurt, oil, lemon juice, turmeric and garam masala then rub the ingredients into the chicken.

Leave to marinate for 4 hours (or it can be left in the fridge overnight).

Place the chicken in a preheated oven at 180C for 20 minutes until the chicken is cooked.

Serve with Indian salad.

Okra (Bindi) Pakora

INGREDIENTS

135g okra (bindi)

FOR THE FILLING
½ tsp turmeric powder (haldi)

1 tsp garam masala

1 heaped tsp green chilli paste

¾ tsp salt

½ tsp dried fenugreek leaves
(methi)

½ tsp cumin seeds (jeera)

1 tsp fresh coriander, chopped

½ tsp lemon juice

PAKORA BATTER
3 heaped tbsp gram flour
(besan)

5 tbsp water

pinch of salt

pinch of carom seeds (ajwain)

oil for deep fat frying

SERVES 2
(Vegetarian)

METHOD

Filling
Place all the ingredients for the filling into a bowl and mix well to combine.

Wash and dry the okra on kitchen paper. Make a slit lengthwise in each one and stuff with the filling mixture. Coat the okra in any remaining mixture.

Batter
Place the gram flour, salt and carom seeds in a bowl and mix.

Add the water and mix to form a smooth batter.

Cooking
Heat the oil in a deep fat fryer to 180C then dip the okra in the batter and deep fry for 3 minutes. Remove for 60 seconds then place back in the fryer and cook until golden brown and crisp.

Spicy Chick Peas (Chana Chaat)

INGREDIENTS

8 tbsp vegetable oil

1 tsp cumin seeds (jeera)

1 onion, chopped

1 tsp ginger and garlic paste

½ tsp salt

½ tsp red chilli powder

1½ heaped tsp tomato purée

1 fresh tomato, chopped

¾ tsp turmeric powder (haldi)

¼ tsp curry powder

400g chickpeas (chana)

2 level tsp tomato ketchup

¼ tsp mint sauce

2 tsp mango chutney

8 tbsp warm water

pinch garam masala, dried fenugreek leaves (methi) and fresh coriander, chopped

SERVES 2
(Vegetarian)

METHOD

Heat the oil in a medium-sized pan and add the onions and cumin seeds. Stir frequently until the onions are golden brown (10 minutes).

Add the ginger and garlic paste, salt, turmeric, curry powder, tomato purée and chopped tomato and red chilli powder, stirring frequently. Once the tomatoes have dissolved, add the chickpeas and stir into the mixture for approximately 6 minutes.

In a separate bowl, put the tomato ketchup, mint sauce and mango chutney and mix together. Add this to the chickpeas and stir for a couple of more minutes.

Add a pinch of garam masala, fenugreek and coriander and mix together.

Serve in a bowl.

Fish Cakes

INGREDIENTS

2 medium potatoes

200g haddock, cod or whiting

½ tsp turmeric powder (haldi)

3 spring onions, chopped

2 green chillies de-seeded and chopped

1.5cm piece of fresh ginger, finely chopped

2 tbsp fresh coriander, chopped

finely grated zest of 1 lemon

juice of 2 lemons

salt and pepper to taste

groundnut oil for frying

SERVES 2

METHOD

Boil the potatoes in salted water until soft. Poach the fish until cooked (5-7 minutes) then drain.

Mash the potatoes and flake the fish into chunks.

Place the fish and the potatoes with the other ingredients in a bowl and mix well to combine.

Add salt and pepper to taste.

Carefully shape into 4 cakes about 2.5cm thick.

Heat a thin layer of oil in a large frying pan and fry the fish cakes on a medium heat for about 5 minutes each side or until golden brown.

Bread Pakora

INGREDIENTS

oil to deep fry

2 slices of bread, halved

9 tbsp gram flour (besan)

175ml water

1 tsp salt

¾ tsp red chilli powder

1½ tsp carom seeds (ajwain)

1 tsp fresh coriander, chopped

SERVES 2
(Vegetarian)

METHOD

Heat oil in a deep fat fryer to 170C.

In a large bowl, mix the gram flour, salt, chilli powder, carom seeds and coriander. Gradually add the water to the bowl and mix to create a smooth batter.

Coat the bread in the batter until completely covered.

Deep-fry the bread until crispy an golden brown. Lift the pakoras from the oil with a slotted spoon when ready and place them on kitchen paper to remove excess oil.

Serve with a chutney (see pages 181-206).

Vegetable Samosa

INGREDIENTS

FOR THE FILLING
oil for deep frying

240g potato, peeled
1 tbsp crushed coriander seeds
(dhania)

1 tbsp vegetable oil

pinch cumin seeds (jeera)

¼ tsp ginger and garlic paste

3 tbsp garden peas

½ tsp salt

½ tsp red chilli powder

½ tsp garam masala

oil for deep frying

FOR THE PASTRY
Two 25cm square pieces of
spring roll pastry cut into 3
equal size strips

Flour and water to make a
paste

SERVES 3
(Vegetarian)

METHOD

Heat oil in a deep fat fryer to 170C.

Dice the potato into small pieces (about 1cm cubes) and boil until soft. Drain and allow to cool.

In a saucepan, heat the oil and add the cumin seeds and ground coriander. Fry for about 1 minute until the cumin has browned then add all the other ingredients for the filling.

Combine all the ingredients, stirring regularly to make sure the mixture does not stick to the pan.

Take 2 strips of the pastry and place one on top of the other, fold one half to form a cone shape and brush underneath the cone with the paste mixture so that it sticks. Fill the cone with the filling, pressing it down. Fold the other half over to make a triangle and seal the outer edges with the paste making sure the samosas are sealed completely.

Deep-fry the samosas in the oil for 4-5 minutes until golden brown, stirring occasionally. Do not allow them to brown too quickly.

Fish (Machi) Pakora

INGREDIENTS

oil for deep frying

400g white fish, sliced

pinch carom seeds (ajwain)

pinch cumin seeds (jeera)

½ tsp salt

1 tsp green chilli paste

½ tsp tikka paste

½ tsp ginger and garlic paste

1½ tsp lemon juice

3 heaped tbsp gram flour (besan)

5 tbsp (approx.) water

SERVES 2

METHOD

Heat oil in a deep fat fryer to 170C.

In a bowl, mix the fish, carom seeds, salt, lemon juice, ginger and garlic paste, cumin seeds, green chilli paste and tikka paste. Leave to marinate for 15 minutes.

Add the gram flour and mix it into the marinade. Gradually add the water to the mixture to make a smooth batter.

Deep-fry the fish until crispy an golden brown. Lift the pakoras from the oil with a slotted spoon when ready and place them on kitchen paper to remove excess oil.

Serve with pakora sauce (see page 181).

Spicy Puffed Rice (Bhel Puri)

INGREDIENTS

1 tbsp tamarind pulp (imli)

100g puffed rice

1 medium tomato, chopped

3 tbsp onion, chopped

2 tbsp fresh coriander, chopped

3 chopped green chillies

1 tbsp crushed roasted cumin seeds (jeera)

½ tsp lemon juice

30g aloo bhujia (available from most Asian shops)

30g bombay mix

1 small potato, cooked and diced into small cubes

coriander chutney

SERVES 4
(Vegetarian)

METHOD

Place the tamarind pulp in a bowl with two tablespoons of hot water and leave for approximately 10 minutes. Squeeze the tamarind pulp through a sieve and reserve the juice.

In a bowl, mix together the puffed rice, chopped tomato, coriander, green chillies, roasted cumin, lemon juice, tamarind juice, aloo bhujia, bombay mix and diced potato.

Stir all the ingredients together and serve with coriander chutney, optional, (see page 193).

MAIN COURSES

Main courses consist of chicken, meat, fish or vegetables.

The great thing about Indian main courses is that you can have any kind of meat, fish or vegetable as they will go with most of the curry sauces. I am not a vegetarian but when I lived in India I didn't miss meat as there were so many different kinds of vegetarian dishes to choose from. Often, if our aunties or uncles come over we keep the main course vegetarian as they prefer not to eat meat.

I have carefully chosen main courses which come from all corners of India including some with Glasgow influences like Chicken Chasni – Glasgow's favourite dish.

Just a wee reminder to make sure you leave plenty of cooking time for lamb as it takes much longer to cook.

Enjoy!

CHICKEN

Karahi Chicken Bhoona

INGREDIENTS

8 tbsp vegetable oil

1 tsp cumin seeds (jeera)

1 large onion, finely chopped

1 large green pepper, sliced

1 heaped tbsp ginger and garlic paste

1 tsp salt

1 tsp red chilli powder

¾ tsp turmeric powder (haldi)

½ tsp curry powder

1 tsp tomato purée

1½ fresh tomatoes, chopped

400g chicken breast, chopped into 2.5cm cubes

200ml warm water

pinch dried fenugreek leaves (methi), fresh coriander and garam masala

1 fresh tomato, cut into wedges

SERVES 2

METHOD

Heat the oil in a large karahi. Add the onion and cumin and fry gently until the onions are golden brown.

Add the sliced green pepper to the pan and cook until soft.

Add the ginger and garlic paste, salt, red chilli, turmeric, curry powder, tomato purée and chopped tomato, stirring frequently. If you feel the mixture is sticking to the pan, a drop of water can be added.

Once the tomatoes have dissolved, add the chicken and stir into the mixture. Keep stirring for about 3 minutes. Add the warm water and stir. Reduce the heat and stir regularly until the chicken is cooked.

Add the fenugreek, coriander and garam masala. Stir and cook for a further 1-2 minutes.

Stir in the tomato wedges and serve.

Chicken Saag on the Bone

INGREDIENTS

100g butter

2 tbsp vegetable oil

½ tsp cumin seeds (jeera)

½ tsp crushed coriander seeds (dhania)

4 garlic cloves, finely chopped

1.5cm piece of fresh ginger, finely chopped

1 small onion, chopped

1 tsp salt

¼ tsp turmeric (haldi)

1½ tsp green chilli paste

500g chicken on the bone. A mixture of thighs and drumsticks, skinned

400g can of Sarson ka Saag (this can be bought from most Asian supermarkets)

1 tbsp dried fenugreek leaves (methi)

SERVES 4

METHOD

Melt the butter and oil in a pan, add the cumin seeds, coriander and garlic and cook for 1 minute.

Add the ginger and cook for a couple of minutes.

Add the onion and cook until lightly browned.

Add the salt, turmeric and green chilli paste and cook for a further 3 minutes.

Add the chicken and cook for 10-15 minutes stirring regularly then add the saag and cook for another 10 minutes.

Add the fenugreek and stir through the mixture before serving.

Chicken Chasni

INGREDIENTS

400g chicken breast, chopped into 2.5cm cubes

FOR THE CHICKEN
8 tbsp vegetable oil

1 tsp cumin seeds (jeera)

1 large onion, chopped into small cubes

1 tbsp ginger and garlic paste

¾ tsp salt

¾ tsp red chilli powder

1½ tsp tomato purée

½ fresh tomato, chopped

1 tsp turmeric powder (haldi)

¾ tsp curry powder

250ml warm water

350ml single cream

FOR THE PATIA SAUCE
2 tbsp mango chutney

2 tbsp tomato ketchup

1 tsp lemon juice

¼ tsp mint sauce

SERVES 2

METHOD

Heat the oil in a medium-sized pan. Add the onions and cumin seeds and stir frequently for about 10 minutes or until the onions are golden brown.

Add the ginger and garlic paste, salt, red chilli, turmeric, curry powder, tomato puree and chopped tomato and stir frequently. If you feel the mixture is sticking to the pan a splash of water can be added.

Once the tomatoes have dissolved, add the chicken and stir into the mixture. Keep stirring for 5-6 minutes.

Add the warm water to the pan and stir. Cover and reduce the heat. Stir regularly until chicken is cooked.

In a bowl, mix the mango chutney, tomato ketchup, lemon juice and mint sauce (patia sauce). Add to the pan, stir and then slowly add the single cream to avoid splitting.

Mix and reduce the sauce until it reaches the desired consistency then serve.

Chicken Biryani

INGREDIENTS

300g basmati rice, washed thoroughly and left to soak in a bowl

8 tbsp vegetable oil

1½ tsp cumin seeds (jeera)

3 bay leaves

3 black cardamom pods

2 5cm cinnamon sticks

1 large onion, sliced

1½ tsp salt

1 tbsp ginger and garlic paste

1 fresh tomato, chopped

¼ tsp turmeric (haldi)

1 tsp garam masala

300g chicken on the bone, a mixture of thighs and drumsticks, skinned

750ml hot water

1 tbsp fresh coriander, chopped

SERVES 2

METHOD

Heat the oil in a pan and fry the cumin seeds, bay leaves, cardamoms and cinnamon sticks for a couple of minutes.

Add the sliced onions and fry until dark brown.

Add the salt, ginger and garlic paste, garam masala, tomato and turmeric and cook until the tomato has dissolved.

Add the chicken and cook for 10-12 minutes.

Now add the water and wait for it to boil, then add the drained rice, lower the heat and cook until most of the water has evaporated.

Sprinkle the coriander on top of the rice, cover with a tight lid. Leave to cook for 4-5 minutes then serve.

Chicken Sharabi

INGREDIENTS

8 tbsp vegetable oil

1 medium onion, finely chopped

1 tsp cumin seeds (jeera)

¾ tsp ground coriander (dhania)

1 tsp curry powder

1 tbsp garlic and ginger paste

1 tomato, finely chopped

200ml water

1 tsp salt

400g chicken breast, chopped into 2.5cm cubes

100ml red wine

1 tbsp green chilli paste

¾ tbsp patia sauce (see below)

2 tbsp coconut cream

½ tsp ground black pepper

pinch fresh coriander for garnish

1 whole green chilli for garnish

PATIA SAUCE
½ tbsp mango chutney

½ tbsp tomato ketchup

¼ tsp lemon juice

¼ tsp mint sauce

SERVES 2

METHOD

Heat the oil in a frying pan. Add the onions and cumin seeds and fry over a medium heat until the onions are golden brown.

Add the turmeric, ground coriander and curry powder and fry for a further 2 minutes.

Add the ginger and garlic paste. Stir, then add the chopped tomato and 2 tablespoons of the water.

Cook until the tomatoes are puréed then add the salt and about 4-5 tablespoons of water so that the mixture does not become too dry.

Add the chicken and cook for 5 minutes, add the red wine, 7 tablespoons of the water, green chilli paste and patia sauce.

Mix well then add the coconut cream and cook until the cream has dissolved. Add the remaining water stir and sprinkle with a pinch of fresh coriander and a pinch of black pepper.

Serve garnished with the whole green chilli.

Chicken Jaipuri

INGREDIENTS

8 tbsp vegetable oil

1 tsp cumin seeds (jeera)

I large onion, chopped into small cubes

1 tbsp ginger and garlic paste

½ tsp salt

1 level tbsp green chilli paste

1½ tsp tomato purée

1 fresh tomato, chopped

1 tsp turmeric powder (haldi)

½ tsp curry powder

400g chicken breast chopped into 2.5cm cubes

150ml warm water

1½ tsp tandoori paste

½ small green pepper, cut into thin wedges

½ small yellow pepper, cut into thin wedges

½ small red pepper, cut into thin wedges

½ small onion, cut into thin wedges

1 tsp dried fenugreek leaves (methi)

1 tbsp fresh coriander, chopped

1 level tbsp coconut cream

SERVES 2

METHOD

Heat the oil in a medium-sized pan. Add the onions and cumin seeds, fry over a medium heat stirring frequently for about 10 minutes or until the onions are golden brown.

Add the ginger and garlic paste, salt, turmeric, curry powder, tomato purée, chopped tomato and green chilli paste, stirring frequently. If you feel the mixture is sticking to the pan a splash of water can be added.

Once the tomatoes have dissolved, add the chicken and stir it into mixture. Stir frequently for 3-4 minutes until the chicken is sealed on all sides.

Add the peppers and onion. Stir, then add 150ml of warm water to the pan and the tandoori paste and stir for another 3-4 minutes until chicken is cooked.

Add the fenugreek, coriander and coconut cream. Stir and cook for a couple of minutes.

Serve in a bowl.

Chicken with Pickle Curry (Achari Chicken)

INGREDIENTS

6 tbsp mustard oil

¼ tsp mustard seeds

½ tsp cumin seeds (jeera)

¾ tsp fenugreek seeds

½ tsp fennel seeds (saunf)

¾ tsp onion seeds (kalonji)

3 garlic cloves, chopped

5cm piece of fresh ginger, chopped

½ medium onion, sliced

1½ tsp salt

½ tsp turmeric powder (haldi)

2 tsp green chilli paste

1 tbsp plain yoghurt

400g chicken breast, chopped into 2.5cm cubes

1 fresh tomato, chopped

1 tbsp fresh coriander, chopped

SERVES 2

METHOD

Heat the oil in a medium-sized pan and add the onion seeds, mustard seeds, fenugreek seeds, cumin seeds and fennel seeds. Wait for the seeds to crackle.

Add the garlic and fry until lightly browned then add the ginger and fry again for a minute.

Add the onion. Cook until caramelised, then add the turmeric and green chilli paste and cook for another 3 minutes.

Now stir in the yoghurt slowly to avoid splitting and cook for a minute.

Add the chicken to the pan and cook for 6-7 minutes or until it is ready, stirring regularly.

Finish off by adding the chopped tomato. Cook for a couple more minutes then add the coriander and serve.

Chicken Curry

INGREDIENTS

8 tbsp vegetable oil

4 medium onions, chopped

4 tbsp plain yoghurt

½ tsp cumin seeds (jeera)

1 tbsp ginger and garlic paste

¾ tsp turmeric powder (haldi)

1 tsp red chilli powder

1¼ tsp salt

8 tbsp tinned chopped tomatoes blended in a food processor

1kg approx. whole chicken, cut into 10 pieces

300ml warm water

7 tbsp cashew nut paste (see page 10)

pinch ground cardamom

pinch mace powder (javantry)

1 tbsp ground coriander (dhania)

pinch garam masala

130ml water

SERVES 4

METHOD

Heat the oil in a large, heavy pan and fry the onions until dark brown.

Place the cooked onions in a food blender, leaving the excess oil in the pan.

Add the yoghurt to the blender with the onions and 130ml of water and blend to a smooth paste. Keep aside for later.

Using the pan with the leftover oil, add the cumin seeds and when the seeds crackle, add the ginger and garlic paste. Cook for a couple of seconds then add a splash of water if the mixture is sticking to the pan.

Add the turmeric and the onion paste. Remove any leftover paste from the blender by adding 4 tablespoons of water and add this to the pan. Cook for a couple of minutes.

Add the red chilli powder and salt. Mix together and cook for a further 5 minutes.

Stir the tomatoes into the pan.

Add the chicken and the 300ml of warm water and cook for 2-3 minutes.

Cover with a lid, reduce the heat and leave to cook, stirring occasionally, for 20 minutes.

Stir in the cashew nut paste and cover. Cook for 5 minutes.

Add the mace and the cardamom. Cover again and cook for a further 10 minutes or until the chicken is cooked.

Garnish with coriander and garam masala before serving.

Chicken in a Pot

INGREDIENTS

1½ tbsp salt

1 tsp turmeric powder (haldi)

1½ tsp red chilli powder

1 tsp garam masala

3 tbsp ginger and garlic paste

juice from ½ a lemon

1½ tbsp plain yoghurt

1kg approx. whole chicken

12 tbsp vegetable oil

3 medium onions, chopped

1 tsp cumin seeds (jeera)

2 fresh tomatoes, chopped

950ml hot water

2 whole green chillies

pinch fresh coriander

pinch dried fenugreek leaves (methi)

SERVES 4

METHOD

Place the salt, turmeric, red chilli powder, garam masala, ginger and garlic paste, lemon juice and yoghurt into a large bowl and mix all the ingredients thoroughly. Make incisions in the chicken and coat with half the marinade. Leave to marinate for half an hour.

Meanwhile heat the oil in a large pot and fry the cumin seeds and onions until golden brown.

Add the leftover marinade to the pot with the tomatoes and cook until the tomatoes have dissolved (approximately 10-15 mins).

Add the chicken and coat with the mixture. Cover with a tight-fitting lid and leave to cook for 30 minutes stirring every 5-10 minutes.

When almost cooked add the water and cook for a further 15 minutes, then add the whole green chillies. Cook until the water has reduced and the sauce has thickened.

Stir in the coriander and dried fenugreek leaves and serve.

Chicken Tikka Masala

INGREDIENTS

8 tbsp vegetable oil

1 onion, finely chopped

1 tsp cumin seeds (jeera)

½ small green pepper, sliced

½ small red pepper, sliced

½ small yellow pepper, sliced

1½ tbsp ginger and garlic paste

½ tsp salt, or to taste

1 tbsp green chilli paste

¾ tsp turmeric powder (haldi)

1 fresh tomato, chopped

1 tsp tomato purée

¾ tsp tandoori paste

8 pieces cooked chicken tikka (see Starters recipe page 44)

100ml water

2 heaped tbsp plain yoghurt

pinch dried fenugreek leaves, fresh coriander and garam masala

SERVES 2

METHOD

Heat the oil in a frying pan. Add the onion and cumin and fry gently for about 10 minutes until the onions are golden brown.

Slice the peppers and add them to the pan. Cook until the peppers are soft.

Add the ginger and garlic paste and stir. Add the salt, green chilli paste, turmeric, fresh tomato, and tomato purée, and stir continuously for about 10 minutes, ensuring the mixture does not stick to the pan.

Add the tandoori paste and pre-cooked chicken tikka. Mix and then add the water if the mixture is too dry or starts to stick. Stir all the ingredient together then add the yoghurt and stir again to combine.

Add a pinch of fenugreek, coriander and garam masala, stir and cook for a further 2-3 minutes on a medium heat.

Serve in a bowl.

Chicken with Cumin (Chicken Jeera)

INGREDIENTS

600g chicken on the bone. A mix of thighs and drumsticks, skinned

2¾ tsp green chilli paste

2 tbsp plain yoghurt

10 tbsp vegetable oil

2 tbsp cumin seeds (jeera)

1 medium onion, chopped

2 tsp ginger and garlic paste

1 tsp salt

½ tsp turmeric powder (haldi)

½ tsp garam masala

2 tbsp fresh coriander, chopped

SERVES 2

METHOD

In a large bowl, coat the chicken with 2 teaspoons of the green chilli paste then coat with the yoghurt and leave to marinate for 15 minutes.

Heat the oil in a large pan. Add the cumin seeds and onions and fry for 2-3 minutes.

Add the ginger and garlic paste, salt, the rest of the green chilli paste, garam masala and turmeric. Cook for about 2 minutes.

Add the marinated chicken and cook for 25-30 minutes. Stir regularly to prevent the mixture from sticking.

Once the chicken is cooked add the coriander and serve.

Chicken Korma

INGREDIENTS

8 tbsp vegetable oil

¾ tsp cumin seeds (jeera)

1 medium onion, finely chopped

1½ tsp ginger and garlic paste

¾ tsp salt

1 level tsp red chilli powder

¾ tsp turmeric powder (haldi)

½ tsp curry powder

1½ tsp tomato purée

½ fresh tomato, chopped

400g chicken breast, chopped into 2.5cm cubes

250ml warm water

2 heaped tbsp coconut cream

350ml single cream

SERVES 2

METHOD

Heat the oil in a medium-sized pan. Add the onions and cumin seeds and stir frequently for about 10 minutes or until the onions are golden brown.

Add the ginger and garlic paste, salt, red chilli, turmeric, curry powder, tomato purée and chopped tomato stirring frequently. If you feel the mixture is sticking to the pan, a splash of water can be added.

Once the tomatoes have dissolved, add the chicken and stir into the mixture. Keep stirring for 3-5 minutes.

Add the warm water to the pan and stir. Cover and reduce the heat. Stir regularly until chicken is cooked.

Add the coconut cream and single cream slowly to prevent splitting. Stir the mixture and reduce until the desired consistency is reached.

Chicken with Green Chillies

INGREDIENTS

400g chicken thighs and drumsticks

1 tbsp green chilli paste

pinch salt

¼ tsp garam masala

8 tbsp vegetable oil

1 tsp cumin seeds (jeera)

1½ onions, chopped

1 fresh tomato, chopped

1½ tbsp ginger and garlic paste

1 tbsp tomato purée

1 tsp turmeric powder (haldi)

1 tsp salt

4 green chillies, chopped

550ml freshly boiled water

3 tbsp fresh coriander, chopped

¼ tsp garam masala

1 whole green chilli

SERVES 2

METHOD

In a bowl, put the chicken, green chilli paste, salt and garam masala. Mix together and leave to marinate for 15 minutes.

In a medium-sized pan heat the oil and add the cumin seeds. Fry for a couple of seconds and then add the onions. Cook for about 10 minutes until the onions are golden brown then add the tomato purée, ginger and garlic paste, turmeric, tomato, salt and green chillies. Cook for 5 minutes, stirring to stop the mixture sticking to the bottom of the pan.

Add the marinated chicken to the pan and mix thoroughly, ensuring the chicken is covered with the sauce, simmer and cook for about 15 minutes, stirring regularly.

Add the water to the chicken. Bring back to the boil then reduce the heat and cook for a further 15 minutes.

Stir in the garam masala and coriander then garnish with the whole green chilli and serve.

LAMB

Lamb Mince Curry with Peas (Keema Mattar)

INGREDIENTS

6 tbsp vegetable oil

½ onion, chopped

¾ tsp cumin seeds (jeera)

1½ tsp ginger and garlic paste

¾ tsp salt

1 tsp tomato purée

½ tsp turmeric powder (haldi)

¾ tsp red chilli powder

1 small green chilli, chopped

½ fresh tomato, chopped

¼ tsp curry powder

135g garden peas

300g minced lamb

100 ml water

pinch dried fenugreek leaves (methi) and fresh coriander

SERVES 2

METHOD

Heat the oil in a pot and add the chopped onion and cumin. Stir the ingredients together and cook for approximately 10 minutes until the onions are soft and golden brown.

Add the ginger and garlic paste, salt, tomato purée, turmeric, red chilli powder, chopped green chilli, chopped tomato and curry powder. Cook for a further 5 minutes then stir in the peas and cook for another 2-3 minutes.

Place the minced lamb in a bowl and add the water. Mix together until the water has been absorbed into the lamb then add it to the pan with the other ingredients. Stir all the ingredients together and cook for a further 15 minutes, stirring occasionally.

Add a pinch of fenugreek and a pinch of coriander. Mix thoroughly then serve.

Lamb Balti

INGREDIENTS

1½ large onions, chopped

400g boneless leg of lamb, cut into 2.5cm cubes

1 heaped tsp cumin seeds (jeera)

2½ litre hot water

7 tbsp vegetable oil

1 tsp salt

1½ tsp red chilli powder

½ tsp turmeric powder (haldi)

1½ tsp blended mixed pickle

¾ tsp tandoori paste

1 tbsp plain yoghurt

1 heaped tbsp ginger and garlic paste

1 tsp tomato purée

½ tsp fresh tomato, chopped

200g tinned chickpeas

1 tbsp fresh coriander, chopped

1 tsp dried fenugreek leaves (methi)

SERVES 2

METHOD

Into a large pan place the onion, lamb and cumin seeds. Add the water and bring to the boil. Cover, turn down the heat and simmer for 1 hour, stirring occasionally. If there is any water left in the pan after the cooking time, increase the heat to allow the water to completely evaporate.

Reduce the heat and stir the oil into the lamb.

Now add the salt, red chilli powder, turmeric, mixed pickle, tandoori paste, yoghurt, ginger and garlic paste, tomato purée and chopped tomato. Mix all of these ingredients well into lamb and cook on a medium heat for another 20 minutes, stirring regularly.

Mix in the chickpeas and cook for a further 5 minutes.

When the lamb is cooked, stir in the coriander and fenugreek and serve.

Lamb Bhoona

INGREDIENTS

7 tbsp vegetable oil

1 large onion, chopped

1 tsp cumin seeds (jeera)

2.5cm cinnamon stick

2 bay leaves

2 black cardamom pods

300g boneless leg of lamb, cut into 2.5cm cubes

1500ml water

1 tbsp ginger and garlic paste

2 tsp tomato purée

1 fresh tomato, chopped

¾ tsp red chilli powder

1 tsp salt

1 tsp turmeric powder (haldi)

¾ tsp curry powder

1 small green chilli, chopped

600ml warm water

1½ tsp fresh coriander

pinch dried fenugreek leaves (methi)

1 fresh tomato, sliced into 4 wedges

pinch fresh coriander to garnish

SERVES 2

METHOD

Heat the oil in a pan and add the onion, cumin, cinnamon, bay leaves and cardamom. Stir well and cook for 3 minutes.

Add the lamb and the 1500ml of water. Stir to combine the ingredients and cook covered for about 30 minutes or until the lamb is half cooked.

Add the ginger and garlic paste, tomato purée, fresh tomato, red chilli powder, salt, turmeric, curry powder and the green chilli. Mix to combine all ingredients, and cook for a further 20 minutes, stirring regularly.

Add the 600ml of water and bring to the boil. Reduce the heat and cook for a further 15 minutes or until lamb is fully cooked.

Add the fenugreek, coriander and the tomato wedges. Stir and cook for 1 minute to allow the tomato to soften slightly.

To serve, arrange the tomato wedges on top and garnish with fresh coriander.

Lamb Chops and Aloo

INGREDIENTS

8 tbsp vegetable oil

1 large onion, chopped

2 tsp cumin seeds (jeera)

1 tsp salt

1 heaped tbsp ginger and garlic paste

½ tsp turmeric powder (haldi)

½ tsp curry powder

½ tsp red chilli powder

1 fresh tomato, chopped

4 green chillies, chopped

½ tsp tomato purée

6 lamb chops

2 medium-sized potatoes, quartered

500ml warm water

SERVES 2

METHOD

Heat the oil in a pan then add the onions and cumin seeds and stir frequently for about 10 minutes or until the onions are golden brown.

Add salt, ginger and garlic paste, turmeric, curry powder and chilli powder and cook for a few minutes.

Add the green chillies, tomato and tomato purée and cook for 10 minutes.

Add the lamb chops and reduce to a medium heat. Continue cooking for about 25 minutes stirring and turning the chops frequently.

Add the potatoes and mix with all the other ingredients. Cook for 15 minutes then add the water, cover and cook until the lamb is tender.

Lamb Jalfrezi

INGREDIENTS

4 tbsp vegetable oil

½ onion, chopped

½ tsp cumin seeds (jeera)

200g boneless leg of lamb, cut into 2.5cm cubes

800ml water

¼ tsp ginger and garlic paste

1 tsp tomato purée

¼ tsp red chilli powder

½ tsp turmeric powder (haldi)

¼ tsp curry powder

½ tsp salt

400ml warm water

2 tbsp plain yoghurt

¼ tsp tandoori paste

200ml single cream

1 tbsp mixed nuts and raisins

1 tbsp coconut cream

SERVES 1

METHOD

Heat the oil in a pan and add the onion and cumin. Stir well and fry for 3 minutes.

Add the lamb and the 800ml of water. Bring to the boil then reduce the heat, cover and allow to simmer gently for about 30 minutes or until the lamb is half cooked.

Add the ginger and garlic paste, tomato purée, red chilli powder, turmeric, curry powder and salt. Mix to combine the ingredients, cover and cook for a further 5 minutes, stirring frequently.

Add the warm water stir and cover. Simmer gently for a further 10 minutes or until the lamb is fully cooked.

Meanwhile, mix the yoghurt until smooth and add the tandoori paste. Combine both ingredients then add to the lamb and mix thoroughly. Cover and cook for a further 5 minutes, stirring occasionally.

Stir in the single cream a tablespoon at a time to keep it from splitting, then add the nut mixture and the coconut cream.

Stir well to combine then serve.

Lamb Masalum

INGREDIENTS

1 whole leg of lamb, about 2kg

FOR THE MARINADE
4 tbsp ginger and garlic paste

2 tbsp green chilli paste

2 tbsp salt

4 tbsp lemon juice

4 tbsp vegetable oil

FOR THE COOKING
10-12 tbsp vegetable oil

2 tbsp cumin seeds (jeera)

7 black cardamom pods

6 bay leaves

2 6cm pieces of cinnamon stick

6 medium onions, chopped

2 tbsp ginger and garlic paste

3 tbsp turmeric powder (haldi)

3 tbsp green chillies, chopped

2 tbsp salt

1 tsp garam masala

7 fresh tomatoes, chopped

6 tbsp plain yoghurt

2litre freshly boiled water

4 tbsp fresh coriander, chopped

2 tbsp dried fenugreek leaves (methi)

2 whole green chillies

SERVES 6

METHOD

For the Marinade
Mix all the ingredients in a bowl.

Make deep cuts in the lamb and push the marinade inside. Rub the rest of the marinade over the lamb and leave it to marinate in the fridge for at least 8 hours or overnight.

For the Cooking
In an extra large pot heat the oil and fry the cardamom, bay leaves, cinnamon and cumin seeds for a couple of minutes. Add the onions and cook for 20 minutes, then add the leg of lamb.

Cook the lamb for 1hour 40 minutes, turning and browning regularly on a medium heat.

Add the ginger and garlic paste, turmeric, chopped green chillies, salt, garam masala and tomatoes. Mix into the lamb and cook until the tomatoes are completely dissolved.

Stir in the yoghurt slowly to avoid splitting and cook for another 15 minutes. Add the freshly boiled water and cook covered on a medium heat for another 1 hour and 45 minutes turning occasionally until the lamb is tender. Reduce the sauce to the desired consistency. Remove any excess oil then stir in the coriander, fenugreek and the two whole green chillies.

Mix through and serve on a large serving plate.

Lamb Kofta & Boiled Egg Curry

INGREDIENTS

FOR THE KOFTAS

2 tsp ginger and garlic paste

1 tsp cumin seeds (jeera)

½ medium onion, finely chopped

1 heaped tsp green chilli paste

2 tbsp fresh coriander, chopped

½ tsp garam masala

¾ tsp salt

400g lamb mince

FOR THE CURRY

8 tbsp vegetable oil

1 medium onion, chopped

1 tsp cumin seeds (jeera)

1 tbsp ginger and garlic paste

1 tsp green chilli paste

1 heaped tsp turmeric powder (haldi)

½ fresh tomato, chopped

pinch garam masala

pinch fresh coriander

¾ tsp salt

5 tbsp tinned tomatoes, blended in a food processor

350ml freshly boiled water

4 hard-boiled eggs

SERVES 2

METHOD

For the Koftas

Place all the ingredients (except the lamb) in a blender and blend until smooth.

Add the blended ingredients to the minced lamb in a bowl. Combine thoroughly and leave to rest for about 10 minutes.

Form the mixture into about 8 medium-sized balls and set aside.

For the Curry

Heat the oil in a pan. Add the onions and cook until soft.

Remove the onions and place them in a blender and blend them to a smooth paste.

Return the onions to the pan. Stir and wait until the oil starts to appear around the sides of the pan.

Now add the cumin seeds to the onion mixture and fry on a medium heat until the onions are lightly browned.

Lower the heat while adding the ginger and garlic paste, green chilli paste, turmeric, salt and tomato and cook for about 5 minutes on a medium heat.

Add the blended tomatoes and cook for a further 5 minutes.

Add the koftas to the pan and leave for a couple of minutes. Gently cover the koftas with the sauce, cook for a further 3 minutes and then stir to ensure the sauce is not sticking to the bottom of the pan.

Cook for a further 5 minutes and then add the freshly boiled water and the eggs. Cook on a medium heat and reduce until the required consistency of sauce is reached.

To finish, add the coriander and garam masala stir then serve.

Lamb Rogan Josh

INGREDIENTS

5 tbsp ghee

1 large onion, chopped

1 tsp cumin seeds (jeera)

300g boneless leg of lamb, cut into 2.5cm cubes

1500ml water

1 tsp salt

1 tbsp ginger and garlic paste

2 tsp tomato purée

¾ tsp red chilli powder

1 tsp turmeric powder (haldi)

½ tsp curry powder

8 tbsp tinned plum tomatoes, blended in a liquidiser

1 fresh tomato, chopped

600ml warm water

250ml single cream

1 tsp cashew powder

1 tsp almond powder

1 tsp peanut powder

2 tbsp coconut cream

pinch dried fenugreek leaves (methi)

2 pinches fresh coriander

SERVES 2

METHOD

Heat the ghee in a medium-sized pan and add the onion and cumin. Stir well and cook for 3 minutes.

Add the lamb and the 1500ml of water. Stir and cover then leave to cook on a medium heat for about 30 minutes or until the lamb is half cooked.

Add the ginger and garlic paste, tomato purée, red chilli powder, turmeric, curry powder and mix to combine all the ingredients.

Add the chopped tomato and the blended tomatoes. Cover and cook for a further 15 minutes stirring frequently.

When the ghee comes to the surface of the sauce add the 600ml of warm water and cover, Cook for a further 15 minutes or until the lamb is fully cooked.

Add the single cream, stirring it in a tablespoon at a time to avoid splitting. Once the sauce has come to the boil add the coconut cream and nut powder and stir again.

Stir in a pinch of fenugreek and coriander.

Garnish with another pinch of coriander and serve.

Lamb Shanks

INGREDIENTS

2 medium-size lamb shanks

½ tbsp garam masala

2 tbsp plain yoghurt

10 tbsp vegetable oil

3 green cardamom pods

2 5cm cinnamon sticks

2 bay leaves

½ tsp cumin seeds (jeera)

1½ medium onions, chopped

½ tsp salt

5 green chillies

1 tsp turmeric powder (haldi)

1½ tbsp ginger and garlic paste

1 tbsp tomato purée

1 fresh tomato, chopped

1litre freshly boiled water

2 sliced green chillies

1 tbsp fresh coriander, chopped

SERVES 2

METHOD

Put the lamb shanks in a large bowl and coat them with the garam masala.

Cover the lamb with the yoghurt and leave to marinate for 20 minutes.

Heat the oil in a large pan then add the green cardamoms, cinnamon sticks, bay leaves and cumin seeds. Fry for a couple of minutes and then add the onion and fry until soft.

Add the salt, green chillies, turmeric, ginger and garlic paste, tomato purée and chopped tomato. Cook for 5 minutes and then add the lamb shanks. Cover the lamb shanks with the mixture and cook on a low heat, stirring consistently to prevent the mixture from sticking to the pan. Cook for another 40 minutes. If the mixture is sticking to the pan a splash of water can be added.

Add the freshly boiled water and return to the boil. Reduce heat, cover and leave to simmer slowly for about 30 minutes or until the lamb is ready and the sauce has thickened.

Add the sliced green chillies and chopped coriander then serve.

South Indian Lamb

INGREDIENTS

1 large onion, sliced

1 tsp cumin seeds (jeera)

300g boneless leg of lamb, cut into 2.5cm cubes

7 tbsp vegetable oil

1 tsp ginger and garlic paste

¾ tsp turmeric powder (haldi)

½ tsp curry powder

1 tbsp tomato purée

1 tsp salt

1½ tbsp red chilli powder

1 tsp Kashmiri red chilli powder (Degi Mirch)

2.25litres freshly boiled water

3 tbsp sugar

2 tbsp garlic paste

100ml vinegar

2 tsp cornflour

1 tbsp fresh coriander

1 fresh tomato, cut into wedges

pinch fresh coriander

SERVES 2

METHOD

Place the onion and cumin in a pan and add the lamb. Cover and cook for 5 minutes on a medium heat, checking to make sure the mixture is not sticking.

Stir the lamb and cook, covered, for a further 20 minutes, stirring regularly.

Add the oil to the lamb and cook for another 5 minutes.

Add the ginger and garlic paste, turmeric, curry powder, tomato purée, salt, red chilli powder and Kashmiri red chilli powder.
Stir all the ingredients in with the lamb and cook uncovered for 10 minutes.

Add the freshly boiled water, sugar and garlic paste. When the water returns to the boil, cover, reduce the heat and cook until the lamb is tender. This should take about 1 hour and 20 minutes.

At the end of the cooking period put the vinegar and cornflour in a bowl and mix to a paste. Stir the paste slowly into the lamb mixture then add the coriander and continue stirring until the sauce thickens.

To serve, put the tomato wedges on the top and garnish with a pinch of coriander.

FISH

Spicy Sea Bass

INGREDIENTS

1 whole sea bass, head removed, gutted and descaled. About 240g

1 tsp green chilli paste

3 tbsp vegetable oil

¼ tsp carom seeds (ajwain)

1 egg

1 tsp cornflour

1 tsp gram flour (besan)

1 tsp salt

½ tsp red chilli powder

pinch dried fenugreek leaves (methi)

pinch garam masala

1 tbsp ginger and garlic paste

½ tsp lemon juice

pinch fresh coriander

SERVES 1

METHOD

Preheat the oven to 180C.

Coat the sea bass with the green chilli paste and leave to rest for 3 minutes.

Combine all the other ingredients in a bowl with 2 tablespoons of the oil and coat the sea bass with the mixture.

Leave to rest for another 30 minutes.

Place a piece of parchment paper coated with the remaining tablespoon of oil on a baking tray and place the fish on top.

Roast in the oven, basting with the remaining mixture, for 10-12 minutes or until the fish flakes easily with a fork.

Bengali King Prawn Curry (Machar Jhol)

INGREDIENTS

8 tbsp vegetable oil

¼ tsp mustard seeds

pinch fenugreek seeds

½ tsp cumin seeds (jeera)

¼ tsp onion seeds (kalonji)

¼ tsp carom seeds (ajwain)

pinch fennel seeds (saunf)

2 medium onions, chopped

1 tbsp ginger and garlic paste

¼ tsp turmeric powder (haldi)

¼ tsp red chilli powder

¾ tsp salt

8 tbsp tinned tomatoes, blended in a liquidiser

200ml warm water

6 raw king prawns, shelled and deveined

1 whole dried red chilli

pinch garam masala

SERVES 2

METHOD

Heat the oil in a karahi and fry the mustard seeds, fenugreek seeds, fennel seeds, cumin seeds, onion seeds, and carom seeds. Wait for the seeds to crackle.

Add the onions and fry until dark brown.

Add the ginger and garlic paste, turmeric, red chilli powder and salt and stir for a few minutes. Add 4 tablespoons of the warm water and cook for a couple of minutes.

Add the blended tomatoes and stir and cook on a medium heat for 3-4 minutes.

Now add the king prawns and the whole dried red chilli and stir for 2 minutes then add the remaining water, cover and continue cooking for approximately 3 minutes or until the prawns are cooked. Avoid overcooking the prawns or they will quickly become tough and rubbery.

Serve with a garnish of garam masala.

Goanese Fish

INGREDIENTS

300g firm white fish, cut into chunks

FOR THE MARINADE
pinch salt
pinch turmeric powder (haldi)
1tsp lemon juice

FOR COOKING
6 tbsp vegetable oil
1 tsp cumin seeds (jeera)
5 garlic cloves, crushed
2.5cm piece of fresh ginger, chopped
½ onion, roughly chopped
1 tsp turmeric powder (haldi)
1 tsp curry powder
1 tsp ground coriander (dhania)
1 fresh tomato, roughly chopped
160g tinned plum tomatoes, blended in a liquidiser
1 tsp salt
1 tsp green chilli paste
175ml water
7 heaped tbsp dessicated coconut
½ tsp ginger and garlic paste
6 mustard seeds
1 tsp tomato purée
9 tbsp coconut milk
1½ tbsp sugar
6 curry leaves

SERVES 2

METHOD

For the Marinade
Place the marinade ingredients in a bowl. Add the fish and coat well then leave in the fridge for 10 minutes to marinate.

For Cooking
Heat 4 tablespoons of the oil in a frying pan until sizzling. Add the cumin seeds and the crushed garlic and ginger. Stir, then add the onion and cook on a high heat until the onions are golden brown.

Add the turmeric, curry powder, ground coriander, chopped tomato, puréed tomatoes, salt and green chilli paste and stir them together. Add 6 tablespoons of water, lower the heat and cook for 5 minutes stirring frequently.

Add another 9 tablespoons of water to the sauce then bring it to the boil and cook for a further 2-3 minutes.

Remove the pan from the heat and put the sauce in a liquidiser with the dessicated coconut and 10 tablespoons of water. Blend until the mixture is smooth and begins to thicken which should take 2-3 minutes. Pour the mixture into a container and keep to one side.

Heat the remaining 2 tablespoons of oil in a clean frying pan. Add the ginger and garlic paste and fry for 1 minute before adding the curry leaves, mustard seeds and tomato purée.

Stir the ingredients together then add the sauce from the container. Cook over a low heat for 1 minute, add the fish, and coconut milk, stir through then add the sugar. Bring to the boil and cook for a further 2-3 minutes.

Place in a bowl and serve.

Salmon Curry

INGREDIENTS

4 salmon fillets, 120g each

FOR THE MARINADE

½ tsp roasted cumin seeds
(jeera)
¼ tsp garam masala
2 tbsp tomato purée
1 tbsp ginger and garlic paste
¼ tsp turmeric powder (haldi)
2 tsp lemon juice
2 tbsp vegetable oil
1 tsp salt
¼ tsp dried fenugreek leaves
(methi)

FOR COOKING

7 tbsp vegetable oil
1 clove of garlic, chopped
1 2.5cm piece of fresh ginger,
sliced
1½ medium onions, chopped
1 tsp ginger and garlic paste
1½ tsp green chilli paste
1 tsp salt
1 heaped tsp turmeric powder
(haldi)
1 heaped tsp ground coriander
(dhania)
1 heaped tbsp tomato purée
2 fresh tomatoes, chopped
800ml hot water
2 tbsp coconut powder
2 tbsp tamarind pulp (imli)
pinch mustard seeds
8 curry leaves
1½ tbsp sugar

METHOD

For the Marinade

Place all the ingredients for the marinade in a bowl and mix them together. Add the salmon fillets and leave to marinate for 30 minutes.

For Cooking

Heat 5 tablespoons of the oil in a pan and fry the garlic and ginger for 1-2 minutes. Add the onions and fry until golden brown.

Add the ginger and garlic paste, green chilli paste, salt, turmeric, coriander, tomato purée and chopped tomatoes and mix them all together.

Cook for 20 minutes then add half the hot water and bring to the boil. Cook for a couple of minutes and then remove from the heat.

Stir the coconut powder into the pan then blend the mixture into a smooth paste using a food processor.

Soak the tamarind pulp in enough boiling water to cover it and leave to stand for 15-20 minutes until softened.

In a separate pan add 2 tablespoons of oil and fry the mustard seeds. When they start to crackle, add the curry leaves and fry for 1 minute.

Add the smooth paste to the pan with the remaining hot water. Stir, then add the salmon marinade to the mixture. Stir in the sugar and mix gently to combine.

Cook salmon for 10-15 minutes until cooked through.

Squeeze the tamarind pulp through a fine sieve and add 2 tablespoons of the juice to the salmon. Mix and serve.

SERVES 4

Fish cooked on a Griddle (Tava Machi)

INGREDIENTS

½ tsp cumin seeds (jeera), roasted

¾ tsp tomato purée

¾ tsp tandoori paste

½ tsp English mustard

¼ tsp mint sauce

¾ tsp ginger and garlic paste

¾ tsp green chilli paste

pinch chaat masala

½ tsp dried fenugreek leaves (methi)

1 tsp ginger juice (see page 11).

½ tsp salt

1½ tsp lemon juice

2 tsp vegetable oil

270g haddock fillet, cut Into 6 pieces

½ tsp cornflour

SERVES 2

METHOD

Place all the ingredients apart from the fish and the cornflour in a bowl and mix thoroughly.

Add the fish pieces and coat them with the mixture.

Leave to marinade for 20 minutes.

Brush the tava with oil and wait for it to heat up. Dust the fish with the cornflour, then place the fish on the tava and cook on a medium heat for approximately 2½ minutes.

Turn the fish over and cook for a further 2½ minutes. Turn again until the fish is cooked thoroughly.

Serve with rice and tomato salad.

VEGETABLE

Potato and Cauliflower Curry (Aloo Gobi)

INGREDIENTS

4 tbsp vegetable oil

½ onion, chopped

1 tsp cumin seeds (jeera)

½ tsp salt

¼ tsp red chilli powder

½ tsp turmeric powder (haldi)

1 tsp ginger and garlic paste

½ tsp fresh tomato, chopped

1 tsp tomato purée

100g diced potato

50g cauliflower

125ml freshly boiled water

pinch dried fenugreek leaves (methi)

a few sprigs of fresh coriander

SERVES 2

METHOD

Fry the onion in the oil with the cumin seeds and cook until the onions are soft.

Add the salt, red chilli powder, turmeric and ginger and garlic paste. Stir to mix all the ingredients together.

Add the chopped tomato and cook for a minute or two then add the tomato purée. Stir and cook for another 2 minutes or so.

Add the potato and cook until it begins to soften, stirring occasionally.

Add the cauliflower, stir and cook covered for 5 minutes.

Add the water and continue to cook covered for a further 5 minutes or until the potatoes are cooked, stirring frequently.

Stir in a pinch of fenugreek and serve with a garnish of coriander leaves.

Traditional Indian Daal (Tarka Daal)

INGREDIENTS

500ml water

75g orange lentils

3 tbsp ghee

3 garlic cloves, finely chopped

2.5cm piece of fresh ginger, finely chopped

¼ onion, chopped

½ tsp cumin seeds (jeera)

1 tsp salt

1 tsp turmeric powder (haldi)

1 tsp green chilli paste

½ fresh tomato, chopped

½ tsp tomato purée

pinch dried fenugreek leaves (methi) and fresh coriander

¼ fresh tomato, roughly chopped

SERVES 4

METHOD

Boil the water in a saucepan and add the lentils with 1 tablespoon of the ghee. Mix and leave to simmer, covered on a medium heat until soft.

In a frying pan, melt the other 2 tablespoons of ghee and fry the garlic and ginger until browned.

Add the chopped onion and the cumin seeds. Fry until the onion is well browned.

When the onions are browned add the remaining ingredients except the fenugreek, quarter tomato and coriander. Stir all the ingredients together then add to the pan of cooked lentils. Stir then add the fenugreek, coriander and the chopped tomato.

Mix through and serve.

Home Made Saag (Desi Saag)

INGREDIENTS

300g spinach leaves, chopped
(palak)

200g broccoli, cut into
medium-sized florets

10 brussels sprouts

water (enough to just cover
the vegetables for boiling)

2 tbsp dried fenugreek leaves
(methi)

4½ heaped tbsp ghee

4 garlic cloves, chopped

5cm piece of fresh ginger,
chopped

6 green chillies

1 tsp cornmeal flour

1 knob of ghee

SERVES 2

METHOD

Take a large pan and boil the spinach, broccoli, brussel sprouts,
2 tablespoons of the ghee and the salt. Cover and simmer on a low
heat for about 1 hour.

Using a potato masher, mash the vegetables until they are smooth.

Add the cornmeal gradually to the vegetables stirring at the same
time. This will thicken the saag.

In a separate frying pan add 2 tablespoons of ghee and fry the
garlic. Cook for a minute and then add the ginger and fry for
2 minutes. Add the chopped green chillies and fry for a further
2 minutes.

Add this mixture to the saag and mix together.

Serve with a knob of ghee.

Gramflour Pakora Dumpling (Kuree)

INGREDIENTS

FOR THE GRAM FLOUR GRAVY

1 tbsp vegetable oil

3 tbsp gram flour (besan)

3 tbsp plain yoghurt

1½ litres water

FOR THE MASALA

5 tbsp vegetable oil

1 whole dried red chilli

¼ tsp mustard seeds

8 curry leaves

½ tsp cumin seeds (jeera)

3 garlic cloves, chopped

2.5cm piece of fresh ginger, chopped

½ medium onion, chopped

¼ tsp turmeric powder (haldi)

2 tsp salt

¼ tsp chilli powder

3 whole green chillies

6 pieces vegetable pakoras (see page 15)

pinch fried fenugreek leaves (methi)

1 tbsp fresh coriander, chopped

SERVES 2

METHOD

For the Gram Flour Gravy

Mix the gram flour and yoghurt in a bowl and stir both ingredients to form a smooth paste.

Heat a tablespoon of oil in a pan and add the gram flour mixture. Add the water and cook for 20 minutes.

For the Masala

While the gravy is cooking, heat 5 tablespoons of oil in a pan. Add the whole red chilli, mustard seeds and curry leaves and stir for 1 minute.

Add the cumin seeds and garlic and stir for a couple of seconds, then add the ginger and stir and cook for a further 2 minutes.

Add the onion and cook until golden brown before adding the turmeric, salt and green chillies and cooking for a further 5-7 minutes.

Add the cooked masala mixture to the gravy mixture and cook for 15 minutes on a medium heat until thickened.

Add the vegetable pakoras and cook for a further 2-3 minutes.

Finish off by stirring in the fenugreek and coriander, then serve.

Potato with Fenugreek (Aloo Methi)

INGREDIENTS

4 tbsp vegetable oil

½ tsp cumin seeds (jeera)

2 garlic cloves, chopped

2.5cm piece of fresh ginger, chopped

½ onion, sliced

1 tsp salt

½ tsp turmeric powder (haldi)

½ tsp curry powder

½ tsp red chilli powder

½ fresh tomato, chopped

1 medium bunch of fresh fenugreek leaves, chopped (methi)

1 small potato cut into 2cm cubes

pinch garam masala

SERVES 2

METHOD

Heat the oil in a pan and add the cumin seeds and garlic cloves. Cook for 1 minute then add the ginger and cook for a further minute before adding the onion and cooking until it turns light brown.

Add the salt, turmeric, curry powder, chilli powder and tomato and cook until the tomato dissolves.

Add the fenugreek and cook for 10 minutes.

Add the potato and cook until the potato is soft.

Finish off with a pinch of garam masala, then serve.

Punjabi Eggs

INGREDIENTS

3 tbsp vegetable oil

½ tsp cumin seeds (jeera)

1 bay leaf

1 black cardamom

4 black peppercorns

2.5cm cinnamon stick

1 medium onion, chopped

2 whole green chillies

½ tsp tomato purée

200g tinned tomatoes, chopped

½ tsp turmeric powder (haldi)

½ tsp red chilli powder

1 tsp salt

1 heaped tsp ginger and garlic paste

½ tsp green chilli paste

1 tbsp fresh coriander, chopped

4 eggs

pinch garam masala

pinch cumin seeds (jeera)

SERVES 4

METHOD

Heat the oil in a large frying pan, add the cumin seeds, cardamom, black peppercorns, cinnamon and bay leaf and fry for a minute, then add the onion and fry until browned.

Add the whole green chillies and stir, then add the tomato purée and stir again for 1 minute.

Lower the heat, then add the turmeric, red chilli, salt, ginger and garlic paste and green chilli paste and fresh coriander. Stir for a few minutes till well mixed and all the spices have infused. Add the chopped tomatoes and stir until oil starts to rise to the top of the sauce.

Break the eggs on top of mixture, sprinkle a pinch of cumin seeds and garam masala all over and cover for 30 seconds.

Remove the cover and serve.

Crispy Savoury Pancake (Dosa)

INGREDIENTS

FOR THE DOSA

150g basmati rice
50g black lentils (urad daal)
200ml water
½ tsp fenugreek seeds

FOR THE POTATO FILLING

2 medium potatoes
2 tbsp mustard oil
pinch mustard seeds
6 curry leaves
½ tsp turmeric powder (haldi)
½ tsp curry powder
1 tsp salt
1 tbsp garden peas

FOR THE SAMBAR SAUCE

1200ml hot water
50g chana daal
½ tsp turmeric powder (haldi)
pinch mustard seeds
35g baby eggplant (aubergine), chopped
35g baby Indian pumpkins (tinda), peeled and chopped
35g baby squash, peeled and chopped
1 garlic clove, finely chopped
½ fresh plum tomato, chopped
2 stems of curry leaves
15g green Indian drumsticks, cut into medium-sized lengths
3 tbsp mustard oil
1 tbsp tamarind pulp (imli)
1 tsp sambar mix or curry powder
400ml water
1 tsp salt

SERVES 2

METHOD

For the Dosa

Soak the rice and lentils in a bowl of water overnight.

Drain the rice and lentils and place them in a blender with the water and fenugreek seeds. Blend to form a smooth batter.

Using a non-stick frying pan on medium heat take 100ml of the mixture and spread it evenly and thinly to coat the pan. Cook on one side and when the edges start curling, fill with the potato filling, roll up into a pancake and serve with the sambar sauce. Repeat with the remaining batter to make a second dosa.

For the Potato Filling

Boil the potatoes, cool then roughly mash. Heat the mustard oil in a large frying pan, add the mustard seeds, curry leaves, turmeric, curry powder and salt. Cook for a few seconds then add the potatoes and peas and mix all the ingredients together. Use as a filling for the dosa.

For the Sambar Sauce

Place the hot water in a saucepan, add the chana daal and turmeric and bring to the boil. Cook for approx 35 minutes until the daal is soft. Allow the mixture to cool then place it in a blender and blend until smooth. Keep to one side.

Heat the oil in a pan. Add the mustard seeds and cook for a few seconds until the seeds start to crackle. Add all the vegetables and sauté for 2-3 minutes before adding the sambar mix or curry powder. Cook for a further minute then add the blended daal mixture, the 400ml of water and the salt. Cover and cook on a medium heat until vegetables are soft.

Place the tamarind pulp in a bowl and add just enough boiling water to cover it. Leave to stand for 15-20 minutes until softened. Squeeze the juice from the pulp through a fine sieve and reserve the juice.

When the vegetables are cooked add the tamarind juice and bring back to the boil for a couple of minutes before serving in a separate bowl.

Potato Curry (Aloo Sabzi)

INGREDIENTS

3 tbsp vegetable oil

½ tsp mustard seeds

½ onion, chopped

½ green pepper, sliced

1 heaped tsp ginger and garlic paste

¼tsp onion seeds (kalonji)

3 potatoes, cut into 2.5cm dice

½ tsp turmeric powder (haldi)

½ tsp red chilli powder

½ tsp green chilli paste

1½ tsp salt

200ml hot water

2 tbsp fresh coriander, chopped

½ tsp garam masala

SERVES 2

METHOD

Heat oil in a pan and add the mustard seeds. Wait until they crackle, then add the onion and sweat them together for a few minutes.

Add the green pepper and cook for a couple of minutes, then add the ginger and garlic paste and the onion seeds.

Once the mixture has slightly caramelised add the potatoes and stir. Add the turmeric, red chilli powder, green chilli paste and salt and stir for two minutes making sure the potatoes are well coated with the spices.

Add the hot water, cover and simmer until the potatoes are cooked.

When the potatoes are ready, reduce the liquid until the mixture is only slightly wet.

Stir in the fresh coriander and garam masala and stir. Serve in a bowl.

Aubergine Curry (Bharta)

INGREDIENTS

1 medium aubergine

5 tbsp vegetable oil

½ tsp cumin seeds (jeera)

2 garlic cloves, finely chopped

2.5cm piece of fresh ginger, chopped

1 small onion, sliced

6 green chillies

1 tsp tomato purée

1 tsp salt

½ tsp turmeric powder (haldi)

½ tsp curry powder

½ fresh tomato, chopped

1 tsp dried fenugreek leaves (methi)

1 tbsp fresh coriander, chopped

½ tsp garam masala

SERVES 2

METHOD

Coat the aubergine with about a tablespoon of the oil and put it on a tray in a hot oven (170C) for about 1 hour until soft. Place it in a pan of cold water and when cool remove the skin and mash until smooth.

Heat the rest of the oil in a pan. Add the cumin seeds and garlic and cook for a couple of seconds until the aroma rises. Add the ginger and fry for a further few seconds. Add the onion and fry until lightly browned.

Add the green chillies, tomato purée, salt, turmeric, curry powder and fresh tomato and cook for 4-5 minutes stirring frequently.

Add the mashed aubergine and stir thoroughly into all other ingredients and cook for a further 7 minutes.

Add the fenugreek, coriander and garam masala, mix through then serve.

Black Lentil Curry (Daal Makni)

INGREDIENTS

150g black lentils (urad daal)

½ tsp Kashmiri red chilli powder (degi mirch)

5 tbsp vegetable oil

1½ tbsp ginger and garlic paste

2 tbsp tomato purée

½ tsp red chilli powder

1 tsp salt

4 tbsp single cream

1 tsp fenugreek seeds, dry-roasted

knob of butter

SERVES 4

METHOD

Leave the daal to soak in a bowl of water overnight.

Pour the daal and water into a pan, making sure the dall is covered by the water and bring it to the boil. Add the Kashmiri red chilli powder and 2 tablespoons of the oil. Cover and leave to simmer for 1 hour.

Place a small frying pan on a high heat and put the fenugreek seeds in to dry roast. This should only take a minute or so and when the aroma rises tip the seeds into a bowl to cool.

Heat the rest of the of oil in a frying pan and add the ginger and garlic paste. Fry for a couple of minutes.

Add the tomato purée, red chilli powder and salt and cook for a further 10 minutes. Add to the pan of daal and mix.

Stir the single cream slowly into the daal a tablespoon at a time to prevent it from splitting. Add the roasted fenugreek and stir.

Garnish with a knob of butter and serve.

Okra Curry (Bindi Sabzi)

INGREDIENTS

4 tbsp vegetable oil

1 small onion, sliced

½ tsp cumin seeds (jeera)

½ tbsp salt

1 tsp turmeric powder (haldi)

1 tbsp ginger and garlic paste

1 tsp tomato purée

1 tbsp green chilli paste

1 tsp dried fenugreek leaves (methi)

¼ tsp powdered mango (amchoor)

300g okra (bindi), trimmed and sliced into 2.5cm pieces

2 fresh tomatoes, quartered

SERVES 2

METHOD

Heat the oil in a medium-sized pan and fry the sliced onion and cumin seeds together for 5 minutes.

Stir in the salt, turmeric, ginger and garlic paste, tomato purée, green chilli paste, fenugreek and powdered mango. Cook for a couple of minutes.

Add the okra to the pan and stir it into the mixture. Cook until the okra is tender.

Stir in the tomatoes and cook for a few minutes then serve.

Spicy Potato Curry (Bombay Aloo)

INGREDIENTS

8 tbsp vegetable oil

¾ tsp cumin seeds (jeera)

1 medium onion, chopped into small cubes

2 medium potatoes, chopped into medium-sized pieces

1 tbsp ginger and garlic paste

¾ tsp salt

2 tsp green chilli paste

1½ tsp tomato purée

1 fresh tomato, chopped

1 level tsp turmeric powder (haldi)

¼ tsp curry powder

600ml warm water

3 tbsp plain yoghurt

pinch dried fenugreek leaves (methi)

pinch fresh coriander

SERVES 2

METHOD

Heat the oil in a medium-sized pan. Add the onions and cumin and stir frequently for about 10 minutes or until the onions are golden brown.

Add the ginger and garlic paste, tomato purée, turmeric, curry powder, green chilli paste and chopped tomato stirring frequently. Cook for approximately 10 minutes.

Add the potatoes making sure they are well coated with the mixture. Reduce the heat and cover. Stir regularly making sure the mixture does not stick to the bottom of the pan. Cook for 3 minutes.

Stir in the yoghurt a tablespoon at a time to prevent it from splitting. Stir and cook for 5 minutes, then add water to the pan and cook for a further 10 minutes or until the potatoes are soft.

Add a pinch of fenugreek and coriander, stir then serve.

Spinach with Indian Cheese (Palak Paneer)

INGREDIENTS

3 tbsp ghee

2.5cm piece of fresh ginger, chopped

2 garlic cloves, chopped

½ tsp cumin seeds (jeera)

½ onion, chopped

¼ tsp salt

1 tsp green chilli paste

¼ tsp garam masala

100g spinach (palak), finely chopped

175ml water

100g paneer

oil for deep frying

SERVES 2

METHOD

Heat the ghee in a pan and fry the garlic, ginger and cumin until soft. Add the onion and cook until browned.

Add the salt and green chilli paste and mix. Cook for a couple of minutes then add the garam masala. Stir again and cook for another 3-4 minutes.

Now add the spinach to the pan and combine it with all the other ingredients until soft. Add 100ml water and cook gently, stirring frequently.

Meanwhile deep fry the paneer until golden, drain and add it to the pan with the other ingredients.

Add the remaining water and cook for a further 3-4 minutes until the consistency is quite dry.

Scrambled Egg (Egg Bhurji)

INGREDIENTS

4 tbsp vegetable oil

½ medium onion, chopped

½ tsp cumin seeds, (jeera)

1 tbsp ginger and garlic paste

1 fresh tomato, chopped

3 green chillies chopped

½ tsp salt

4 eggs

¾ tsp turmeric powder (haldi)

pinch fresh coriander, chopped

SERVES 2

METHOD

Heat the oil in a pan and fry the cumin seeds for 1 minute.

Add the onion and fry for about 5 minutes until lightly browned.

Add the ginger and garlic paste, tomato, green chilli, turmeric and salt and cook for 5 minutes.

Beat the eggs in a bowl then add them to the pan. Cook on a very low heat, mixing continuously until the eggs are scrambled and cooked.

Add a pinch of coriander and serve.

ACCOMPANIMENTS

All curries are eaten with an Indian bread or with rice. Rotis are made to a very simple recipe but practice is required to get them as round as possible. Make sure the griddle is nice and hot and have your tongs ready!

It's the smell of the butter on rotis which is the signal call to my boys that dinner is ready – you won't have to shout: the aroma fills the house.

Make sure you buy chapati flour when making most of the breads, or self-raising flour for nan. All local Indian shops will stock them both.

For rice, use only basmati as its fragrance combines beautifully with spicy food.

All the popular breads are in this section so enjoy making them!

Most of the chutneys and sauces can be used to complement either a starter or a main course. Raita, for example, can be eaten with a spicy main course to cool the palate, but can also be used as a dipping sauce with starters such as kebabs and samosas.

RICE DISHES

Pilau Rice

INGREDIENTS

4 tbsp vegetable oil

¼ onion, sliced

1 tsp cumin seeds (jeera)

2 bay leaves

2 black cardamom pods

2 2.5cm cinnamon stick

½ tsp salt

½ tsp garam masala

375ml freshly boiled water

150g basmati rice, washed thoroughly and left to soak in a bowl

SERVES 2

METHOD

Heat the oil in a saucepan and fry the onion with the cumin seeds until the onions are soft. Add the bay leaves, cardamoms and cinnamon and cook for a further 4-5 minutes until the onions are golden brown.

Mix in the garam masala and salt and stir for 2 minutes.

Add the water to the saucepan and bring it back to the boil. Drain the rice, add it to the pan and bring back to the boil again. Reduce the heat to medium and cook until almost all the water has been absorbed into the rice.

Cover with a tight-fitting lid and reduce the heat to a minimum. Cook for a further 5-7 minutes.

Remove the pan from the heat and leave it to stand covered for 5 minutes.

Fluff the rice up using a fork to separate the grains and serve.

Lamb Pilau Rice

INGREDIENTS

8 tbsp vegetable oil

4 black cardamom pods

3 cloves

5 bay leaves

4 2.5cm cinnamon sticks

1 medium onion, sliced

400g leg of lamb, bone in, chopped

2 tsp salt

½ tsp garam masala

1450ml freshly boiled water

300g basmati rice, washed thoroughly and left to soak in a bowl

1½ tsp cumin seeds (jeera)

SERVES 2

METHOD

Heat the oil in a pan. Add the cardamoms, cloves, cumin, bay leaves and cinnamon and fry for a couple of minutes before adding the onions. Continue frying until the onions are soft.

Add the lamb and brown it on all sides. Cover, and stir occasionally for 25 minutes.

Add the salt and garam masala. Stir for 2 minutes then add 700ml of the water and bring back to the boil. Reduce the heat to medium, cover and cook for about 20 minutes, ensuring all the water has evaporated.

Add the remaining 750ml of water and bring back to the boil. Drain the rice, add it to the pan and bring back to the boil again. Reduce the heat to medium and cook until almost all the water has been absorbed into the rice.

Cover with a tight-fitting lid and reduce the heat to a minimum. Cook for a further 5-7 minutes.

Remove the pan from the heat and leave it to stand covered for 5 minutes.

Fluff the rice up using a fork to separate the grains and serve.

Vegetable Pilau Rice

INGREDIENTS

¼ onion, sliced

4 tbsp vegetable oil

1 tsp cumin seeds (jeera)

2 bay leaves

2 black cardamom pods

2 2.5cm cinnamon sticks

½ tsp salt

½ tsp garam masala

1 cauliflower floret, chopped

2 tbsp frozen peas

375ml freshly boiled water

150g basmati rice, washed thoroughly and left to soak in a bowl

SERVES 2

METHOD

Fry the onion in the oil with the cumin seeds and cook until onions are soft. Add the bay leaves, cardamoms and cinnamon and cook for a further 4-5 minutes until the onions are golden brown.

Add the cauliflower, peas, garam masala and salt and mix them together.

Add the water to the saucepan and bring it back to the boil. Drain the rice, add it to the pan and bring back to the boil again. Reduce the heat to medium and cook until almost all the water has been absorbed into the rice.

Cover with a tight-fitting lid and reduce the heat to a minimum. Cook for a further 5-7 minutes.

Remove the pan from the heat and leave it to stand covered for 5 minutes.

Fluff the rice up using a fork to separate the grains and serve.

BREADS

Nan Bread

INGREDIENTS

100g self-raising flour

5 tbsp warm water

1 tbsp vegetable oil

¼ tsp salt

pinch black onion seeds
(kalonji) optional

ghee for brushing optional

SERVES 2

METHOD

Place the flour, salt and kalonji (if using) in a bowl and add the water gradually, enough to mix to form a soft pliable dough.

Turn the dough out onto a floured surface and knead until it is smooth and elastic.

Add the tablespoon of oil and gradually fold it into the dough.

Place the dough back in the bowl, cover with clingfilm and leave it to rest in a warm place for 3 hours.

Preheat the tava and the grill so that they are very hot.

Sprinkle some flour on a work surface, divide the dough into two equal size balls and roll them out. Then, using some oil on the finger-tips, pull each nan into a teardrop shape approximately 20cm long.

Place the nan on the tava and cook the bottom first (wait for it to start browning), then place the tava with the nan under the grill until the surface of the nan begins to blister.

Brush with ghee or butter before serving (optional).

Potato Paratha (Aloo Paratha)

INGREDIENTS

200g chapati flour

10-12 tbsp water

½ tsp vegetable oil

1 medium potato, boiled

2 green chillies, chopped

1 tbsp fresh coriander

1 tsp dried fenugreek leaves (methi)

½ tsp cumin seeds (jeera)

1 tsp salt

¼ tsp garam masala

2.5cm piece fresh ginger, grated

1 tbsp ghee or butter

SERVES 2

METHOD

Place the flour in a deep bowl and make a well in the centre.

Add the water gradually, enough to mix to form a soft pliable dough. Knead the dough in the bowl until it is smooth then coat it with the oil.

Wrap the dough in clingfilm and leave in the bowl to rest at room temperature for 15 minutes.

Place the potato in another bowl and mash, then add the green chillies, coriander, fenugreek, cumin seeds, salt, garam masala and ginger and mix together thoroughly.

Put the tava or a heavy-based frying pan over a medium heat and leave it to heat up.

Divide the dough into two equal portions, and roll each one into a ball. Dip one of the balls into some flour and roll it out to make a 10cm diameter circle.

Put half of the potato mixture into the centre and seal by pulling the edges of the rolled out dough back into the centre.

Dip the ball back into the flour and roll it out again. This time it should be about 20cm in diameter.

Place the paratha on the tava and leave it for 5-7 seconds to brown before turning it over to brown on the other side.

Turn again and brush the paratha with the ghee. Turn and brush the other side.

Keep this process going until the paratha is crispy. Keep it warm under a tea towel while the second paratha is being made.

Chapati

INGREDIENTS

200g chapati flour

10-12 tbsp water

½tsp vegetable oil

SERVES 4

METHOD

Place flour in a deep bowl and make a well in the centre.

Add the water gradually, enough to mix to form a soft pliable dough. Knead the dough in the bowl for 10 minutes until it is smooth then coat it with the oil.

Wrap the dough in clingfilm and leave in the bowl to rest at room temperature for 15 minutes.

Put the tava or a heavy-based frying pan over a medium heat and leave it to heat up.

Divide the dough into four even portions. Sprinkle some flour on a work surface, then take a portion of the dough and roll it into a circle about 15cm diameter.

Put the chapati on the tava and leave it for 4-5 seconds to brown, then turn to brown the other side. Turn over the chapati again and using a chapati press or a clean tea towel folded up, apply gentle pressure to the chapati in several places to heat it and encourage it to puff up like a balloon.

Brush the hot chapati with ghee or butter and leave covered in a tea towel until all the chapatis are cooked.

Coriander Paratha

INGREDIENTS

200g chapati flour

10-12 tbsp water

½ tsp vegetable oil

1 tbsp ghee or butter

2 tbsp fresh coriander, chopped

pinch salt

pinch red chilli powder

SERVES 2

METHOD

Place the flour in a deep bowl and make a well in the centre.

Add the water gradually, enough to mix to form a soft pliable dough. Knead the dough in the bowl until it is smooth then coat it with the oil.

Wrap the dough in clingfilm and leave in the bowl to rest at room temperature for 15 minutes.

Put the tava or heavy-based frying pan over a medium heat and leave it to heat up.

Divide the dough into two equal portions, and roll each one into a ball. Dip one of the balls into some flour and roll it out to make a 10cm diameter circle.

Place half the coriander, salt and red chilli powder in the centre and seal by pulling the edges of the rolled out dough back into the centre to form another ball.

Dip the ball back in the flour and roll it out again. This time it should be about 20cm in diameter.

Place the paratha on the tava and leave it for 5-7 seconds to brown, then turn to brown the other side.

Turn again and brush the paratha with the ghee. Turn and brush the other side then turn again.

Keep this process going until the paratha is crispy. Keep it warm under a tea towel while the second paratha is being made.

Maki Di Roti

INGREDIENTS

200g fine cornmeal flour

18 tbsp hot water

1 tbsp butter or ghee

SERVES 3

METHOD

Place the flour in a bowl. Add the water gradually, enough to mix to form a soft pliable dough,

Knead the dough in the bowl for 10 minutes until it is smooth and elastic. This needs to be done just when you are ready to make the rotis.

Now take a tea towel and lay it on a work surface. Divide the dough into four portions and roll each one into a ball.

Place a ball on the cloth, then put some water on your fingers and press down the ball to flatten it. Next, place a piece of clingfilm over the dough ball and press again, rotating it until it looks like a pancake, about 10cm in diameter.

Put the tava or heavy-based frying pan over a medium to high heat and leave it to heat up.

Lift the roti gently to avoid breaking, place it on the tava and let it cook on one side. Turn and do the same for the other side, repeating the process until the roti becomes crispy and golden yellow with brown spots, (about 30 seconds per side). Put the hot rotis under a tea towel in a warm place until they have all been cooked.

Spread one side with the butter or ghee before serving.

Paratha

INGREDIENTS

200g chapati flour

10-12 tbsp water

½ tsp vegetable oil

4 tsp approx. ghee or butter

SERVES 2

METHOD

Place the flour in a deep bowl and make a well in the centre.

Add the water gradually, enough to mix to form a soft pliable dough. Knead the dough in the bowl for 10 minutes until it is smooth then coat it with the oil.

Wrap the dough in clingfilm and leave in the bowl to rest at room temperature for 15 minutes.

Put the tava or a heavy-based frying pan over a medium heat and leave to heat up.

Divide the dough into two equal portions and roll each one into a ball. Dip one of the balls into some flour and roll it into a 15cm diameter circle.

Spread the ghee or butter onto the dough and roll it into a long sausage shape. Working outwards from the centre, coil the dough into a tight circle to give a spiral effect.

Dust the coiled dough with some flour and press it down with the palm of your hand. Roll it out again – this time it should be 20 cm in diameter.

Place the paratha on the tava and leave it for 5-7 seconds to brown, then turn to brown the other side.

Turn again and brush the paratha with the ghee. Turn and brush the other side then turn again.

Keep this process going until the paratha is crispy. Keep it warm under a tea towel while the second paratha is being made.

Poori

INGREDIENTS

150g chapati flour
8 tbsp approx. water
1 tsp vegetable oil
oil for deep frying

SERVES 4

METHOD

Place the flour in a deep bowl and make a well in the centre.

Add the water gradually, enough to mix to form a soft pliable dough. Knead the dough in the bowl until it is smooth.

Wrap the dough in clingfilm and leave in the bowl to rest at room temperature for 15 minutes.

Heat the oil in a deep fat fryer to 190C.

Divide the dough into 4 balls, place some dry flour on a surface, take the ball and roll into a circle approximately 10cm in diameter.

Fry the pooris one at a time in the oil until golden brown. Lift them out with a slotted spoon and drain on a piece of kitchen paper before serving.

White Radish Paratha (Mooli Paratha)

INGREDIENTS

200g chapati flour

10-12 tbsp water

½ tsp vegetable oil

150g white radish (mooli), grated

½ tsp cumin seeds (jeera)

½ tsp salt

¼ tsp garam masala

2 green chillies, chopped

1 tsp fresh coriander, chopped

1 tbsp ghee or butter

SERVES 2

METHOD

Place the flour in a deep bowl and make a well in the centre.

Add the water gradually, enough to mix to form a soft pliable dough. Knead the dough in the bowl for 10 minutes until it is smooth then coat it with the oil.

Wrap the dough in clingfilm and leave in the bowl to rest at room temperature for 15 minutes.

Squeeze the excess liquid from the grated radish and put it in a clean bowl. Mix in the cumin seeds, salt, garam masala, green chillies and coriander.

Put the tava or a heavy-based frying pan over a medium heat and leave it to heat up.

Divide the dough into two equal portions, and roll each one into a ball. Dip one of the balls into some flour and roll it out to make a 10cm diameter circle.

Place half the radish mixture in the centre and seal by pulling the edges of the rolled out dough back into the centre to form another ball.

Dip the ball back into the flour and roll it out again. This time it should be about 20cm in diameter.

Place the paratha on the tava and leave it for 5-7 seconds to brown, then turn to brown the other side.

Turn again and brush the paratha with the ghee. Turn and brush the other side then turn again.

Keep this process going until the paratha is crispy. Keep it warm under a tea towel while the second paratha is being made.

CHUTNEYS & SAUCES

Pakora Sauce

INGREDIENTS

3 level tbsp plain yoghurt

¼ tsp salt

¼ tsp red chilli powder

1½ tbsp tomato ketchup

1 tsp mango chutney

½ tsp mint sauce

5 tbsp approx. milk

pinch black cumin seeds(kala jeera)

SERVES 2

METHOD

Pour the yoghurt into a large bowl. Mix in the salt, red chilli powder and tomato ketchup.

Add the mango chutney and mint sauce and mix again.

Add the milk and stir all the ingredients together. Finally, add the black cumin and mix thoroughly before serving.

Serve with pakora.

Yoghurt and Mint Sauce

INGREDIENTS

3 level tbsp plain yoghurt

½ tbsp ready-made mint sauce

pinch chat masala

pinch roasted cumin seeds (jeera)

½ tsp green chilli paste

¼ tsp sugar

¼ tsp salt

2 tbsp milk

SERVES 2

METHOD

Place all the ingredients except the milk in a large bowl and mix thoroughly.

Add the milk and mix again.

Serve with any starter.

Spiced Onions

INGREDIENTS

¼ onion, finely chopped

3 tbsp tomato ketchup

1 tbsp mango chutney

¼ tsp ready-made mint sauce

pinch black cumin seeds (kala jeera)

pinch fresh coriander, chopped

½ tsp salt

pinch red chilli powder

SERVES 2

METHOD

Put the onion in a medium-sized bowl before adding all the other ingredients.

Mix thoroughly before serving.

Salty Lassi

INGREDIENTS

6 tbsp plain yoghurt

1 tsp salt

150ml milk

pinch fresh coriander, finely chopped

SERVES 1

METHOD

Place all the ingredients in a cocktail shaker and shake.

Pour into a tall glass and serve chilled or place in the fridge until ready to drink.

Mint Chutney

INGREDIENTS

25g tamarind pulp (imli)

70g carrots, chopped

1 tsp fresh ginger, chopped

1½ tsp green chilli paste

10g fresh mint leaves

1 tbsp tomato ketchup

1 tsp mango chutney

½ tsp salt

¼ chaat masala

mint leaf to garnish (optional)

SERVES 2

METHOD

Soak the tamarind pulp in a cup of freshly boiled water for 20 minutes. Tip the pulp into a sieve and using the back of a spoon squeeze the pulp into the sieve and let the juice drip into a bowl.

Put all the remaining ingredients into a food processor and add the tamarind juice.

Whiz until the mixture has been blended into a rough paste.

Garnish with the mint leaf if using, then serve in a small bowl.

Raita

INGREDIENTS

4 tbsp plain yoghurt

¼ tsp ready-made mint sauce

pinch salt

pinch red chilli powder

pinch roasted cumin seeds
(jeera)

milk, if required

1 tbsp onion, chopped

1 tbsp cucumber, chopped

pinch cumin powder

pinch fresh coriander, chopped

SERVES 2

METHOD

Put the yoghurt in a bowl and beat it with a whisk until smooth.

Mix in the mint sauce, salt, red chilli powder, coriander and the roasted cumin seeds.

If the consistency of the raita is too thick a little milk can be added.

Add the chopped onion and cucumber and mix.

Garnish with a pinch of cumin powder and the fresh coriander.

Coriander and Mint Chutney

INGREDIENTS

40g fresh coriander

20g fresh mint leaves

100ml water

2 green chillies

¼ tsp salt

1 tbsp lemon juice

1 tsp sugar

1 small green mango, peeled and stoned

pinch chaat masala

SERVES 2

METHOD

Put all the ingredients in a food processor and blend to make a smooth paste.

Delicious served with kebabs and tikkas.

Dahi Boondi

INGREDIENTS

FOR THE BOONDI
6 tbsp gram flour

pinch salt

water for making batter

oil for deep frying

FOR THE RAITA
6 tbsp plain yoghurt

7 tbsp milk

2 tbsp boondi

¼ tsp salt

¼ tsp black cumin seeds (kala jeera)

pinch garam masala

pinch red chilli powder

pinch garam masala to garnish

SERVES 2

METHOD

For the Boondi
Place the gram flour and salt in a bowl and mix in enough water to make a smooth thin batter.

Heat the oil in a karahi to a medium heat. Pour some of the batter through a round- slotted spoon into the centre of the hot oil and fry until golden brown. Remove them from the fryer using a slotted spoon and place on a piece of kitchen roll to remove any excess oil.

Repeat with the rest of the batter and set the boondi to one side.

For the Raita
Soak the boondi in a bowl of hot water and leave to soften.

Put the yoghurt in another bowl and beat it with a whisk or fork until smooth.

Gradually add the milk and mix again until it reaches the desired consistency.

Add the salt, black cumin, garam masala, chilli powder and mix.

Squeeze the water out of the boondi and add to the yoghurt mixture.

Garnish with another pinch of garam masala and serve.

Coconut Chutney

INGREDIENTS

FOR THE COCONUT PASTE
200g grated coconut

2 green chillies

1 tsp fresh ginger, grated

1 tbsp chana daal, roasted

salt to taste

FOR FRYING
1 tsp vegetable oil

4 tsp mustard seeds

1 whole red chilli

2-3 curry leaves

SERVES 2

METHOD

Place the coconut, green chillies, ginger, roasted chana daal and salt into a blender with a little water and blend to make a fine paste. Set aside.

Heat the oil in a frying pan and add the mustard seeds, red chilli and curry leaves. Fry for a couple of minutes until the seeds crackle.

Remove from the heat and add the coconut paste.

Mix thoroughly and serve hot or cold.

Tomato Salad

INGREDIENTS

½ tsp lemon juice

¼ tsp brown sugar

¼ tsp salt

pinch ground black pepper

1 green chilli chopped

1 tsp fresh coriander, chopped

pinch garam masala

¼ red onion, chopped into small dice

50g cucumber, chopped into small dice

1 fresh tomato, chopped

SERVES 2

METHOD

In a medium-sized bowl mix the lemon juice, brown sugar, salt, black pepper, green chilli, coriander and garam masala.

Combine the onion, cucumber and tomatoes with the rest of the ingredients in the bowl and serve.

Fruit Chutney

INGREDIENTS

¼ red onion, roughly chopped

¼ green pepper, roughly chopped

¼ red pepper, roughly chopped

1 green chilli

½ tsp salt

½ tsp fresh ginger, chopped

pinch chaat masala

2 tbsp tomato ketchup

2 tbsp mango chutney

½ tsp ready-made mint sauce

2 tbsp mixed fruit salad

SERVES 2

METHOD

Place all the ingredients in a food processor and blend into a chutney texture.

Delicious with pakora and kebabs.

Tomato Chutney

INGREDIENTS

30g fresh yellow chickpeas (channa daal)

5 fresh tomatoes, skinned

8 tbsp vegetable oil

1 medium onion, chopped

½ tsp red chilli powder

5 garlic cloves, chopped

salt to taste

pinch asafoetida (hing)

½ tsp turmeric powder (haldi)

3 red chillies

8 curry leaves

¼tsp mustard seeds

SERVES 2

METHOD

Soak the chickpeas in a bowl of cold water for 45 minutes and leave to one side.

Boil the tomatoes in a pan of water until soft, remove the skin and keep aside.

Heat 6 tablespoons of the oil in a pan. Add the onion and sauté until transparent.

Drain the chickpeas and add them to the pan with the garlic, red chilli powder, salt, asafoetida, turmeric and the tomatoes and cook for 3 minutes.

Blend the mixture in a food processor then pour it into a bowl and leave to cool.

Heat the remaining oil in a separate frying pan and fry the whole red chillies, curry leaves and mustard seeds for a couple of minutes. Pour the spices over the tomato mixture and serve.

Mango Salad

INGREDIENTS

¼ red onion, finely diced

50g cucumber, chopped

1 small mango, peeled, stoned and finely diced

1 green chilli, chopped

1 tbsp fresh coriander, chopped

1 tbsp mint leaves, chopped

½ tsp plus a pinch chaat masala

juice from half a fresh lime

pinch brown sugar

¼ tsp salt

SERVES 2

METHOD

Mix the onion, cucumber, mango, green chilli, coriander and mint in a bowl.

Sprinkle in the chaat masala and mix.

Stir in the lime juice, sugar and salt and mix again.

Spoon the mixture into a serving dish and garnish with a pinch of the chaat masala and serve.

Onion Chutney

INGREDIENTS

3 medium onions

100g black lentils (urad daal)

2 tbsp tamarind pulp (imli)

½ tsp red chilli powder

salt to taste

8 tbsp groundnut oil

3 red chillies

pinch mustard seeds

2.5cm piece of fresh ginger, chopped

SERVES 2

METHOD

Soak the lentils in a bowl of water for 45 minutes.

Soak tamarind pulp in enough boiling water to cover for 15 minutes. Squeeze the pulp through a sieve while collecting the resulting juice in a bowl and set aside.

Heat 6 tablespoons of the oil in a large frying pan and sauté the onions until they are soft.

Drain and add the lentils, red chilli powder, ginger, salt and tamarind juice and cook for 3-5 minutes.

Blend the mixture in a food processor. Pour the mixture into a bowl and leave it to cool down.

Using the remaining oil in a separate frying pan, fry the whole red chillies, curry leaves and mustard seeds for a couple of minutes.

Pour the spices over the onion mixture and serve.

Mango Lassi

INGREDIENTS

6 tbsp canned mango pulp

4 tbsp plain yoghurt

1 tbsp sugar

100ml milk

SERVES 1

METHOD

Place all ingredients in a medium-sized bowl and whisk them together using a hand blender.

Pour into a tall glass and serve chilled or place in the refrigerator until ready to drink.

DESSERTS

India has a wide variety of tempting and mouth-watering desserts.

In this section I have included various desserts: from kulfi, which is very refreshing and cleanses the palate, to kheer, which is simply an Indian rice pudding.

Indian Sweet Rice (Kheer)

INGREDIENTS

2litre full-cream milk

100g basmati rice

150g sugar

6 green cardamom pods

flaked almonds for garnishing

SERVES 4

METHOD

Put the milk and cardamoms in a non-stick pan and slowly bring to the boil. Add the rice and simmer on a low heat, stirring from time to time to prevent the rice from sticking to the bottom of the pan.

Continue to simmer, stirring occasionally, until the milk has reduced by about half. This may take approximately 1 hour.

Once the mixture has thickened, add the sugar and stir continuously for another 5 minutes.

Garnish with flaked almonds (optional) and serve.

Indian Ice Cream (Kulfi)

INGREDIENTS

2litre full-cream milk

12 green cardamom pods

150g caster sugar

25g flaked almonds (optional)

SERVES 4

METHOD

Place the milk and cardamoms in a large, heavy pan.

Bring to the boil and simmer uncovered for 1 hour or until reduced to about a third of the quantity of milk. Stir continuously to keep the milk from sticking to the pan.

Discard the cardamom pods then stir in the caster sugar and chopped almonds. Mix until the sugar has completely dissolved then leave to cool.

Pour the mixture into a freezer-proof container and place it in the freezer. Take the container out of the freezer and mix every 30 minutes until the mixture is almost solid.

Put the mixture into four kulfi moulds (or small yoghurt pots can be used). Keep the pots in the freezer until required and remove them 10 minutes before serving to allow the kulfi to soften.

Garnish with flaked almonds if using.

Creamy Rice Dessert (Phirni)

INGREDIENTS

1litre milk

50g basmati rice

250g sugar

1 tsp cardamom powder (dhania)

pinch saffron

2 drops rose water

1 tsp pistachio, chopped

2 tsp almonds, chopped

SERVES 2

METHOD

Soak the rice in a bowl of water for 1 hour.

Drain and grind the rice to a coarse paste in a blender.

Put the milk in a heavy-duty saucepan, bring it to the boil then reduce to a low heat.

Add the rice paste and cook for 15 minutes. Add the sugar, cardamom powder, saffron and rose water to the milk.

Cook for 5-7 minutes, stirring continuously and scraping the sides and bottom of the pan to ensure the mixture thickens.

Allow the mixture to cool. Pour it into a decorative dessert bowl and put it in the fridge to set.

Garnish with the pistachio and almonds and serve cold.

Vermicelli Pudding (Saymeeha)

INGREDIENTS

3 tbsp ghee

100g vermicelli

2 green cardamom pods

3 tbsp ghee

500ml full fat milk

100ml single cream

2 tbsp sugar

SERVES 4

METHOD

Melt the ghee in a pan, add the green cardamoms and crumble the vermicelli into the ghee. On a low heat, brown the vermicelli making sure it does not burn.

When the vermicelli has softened stir in the milk and cream.

Bring to the boil and immediately stir in the sugar and leave to simmer uncovered for 5 minutes.

Serve hot or cold.

INDEX

GLOSSARY

Achar	Indian mixed pickle
Ajwain	Carom seeds
Aloo	Potato
Aloo Bhujia	Indian potato and gram flour savoury snack
Amchoor	Powdered dried green mangoes
Atta	Chapati flour
Besan	Gram flour made from chick peas
Bharta	Aubergine flesh
Bhurji	Scrambled eggs
Bindi	Okra or ladyfingers
Boondi	Small pea-like gram flour balls
Chaana Daal	Yellow split chick peas
Chaat Masala	Spice mix
Chana	Chickpeas
Daal	Lentils
Degi Mirch	Kashmiri red chilli powder. Similar to paprika but with a mild hint of chilli
Dhania	Coriander
Dosa	Thin crispy pancake
Garam Masala	A mix of Indian spices
Ghee	Clarified butter
Gobi	Cauliflower
Haldi	Turmeric
Hing	Asafoetida used for flavouring
Imli	Tamarind
Javantry	Mace
Jeera	Cumin
Kala Jeera	Black cumin
Kalonji	Black onion seeds
Karahi	Indian wok
Keema	Minced meat
Kheer	Indian sweet rice
Kofta	Meatballs

GLOSSARY

Kulfi	Indian ice cream
Lassi	Yoghurt-based drink
Machi	Fish
Malai	Creamy
Maki	Cornmeal flour
Mattar	Peas
Methi	Dried fenugreek leaves
Mooli	White radish
Pakora	Deep fried gram flour indian snack
Palak	Spinach
Paneer	Indian cheese
Paratha	Unleavened Indian bread
Phirini	Creamy rice dessert
Poori	Thin fried chapati
Raita	A yoghurt-based dip
Roti	Chapati
Saag	Spinach-based Indian dish
Sambar Mix	Mixture of Indian spices
Sabzi	Vegetable curry
Sameeya	Vermicelli
Samosa	Spiced filled pastry
Saunf	Fennel seeds
Tarka	Base sauce
Tava	Indian flat griddle
Tinda	Baby pumpkin
Urad Daal	Black Lentils. Can also be bought white with the skin removed

WEIGHTS, MEASURES & SERVINGS

STANDARDS LIQUID

1 tsp	=	5ml
1 tbsp	=	15ml
1 fl.oz	=	30ml
1 pint	=	20 fl.oz
1 litre	=	35 fl.oz

STANDARDS SOLID

1 oz	=	30g
1 lb	=	16 oz
1g	=	0.35 oz
1 kg	=	2.2 lb

LIQUID CONVERSIONS

Metric	Imperial
15ml	1/2 fl.oz
30ml	1 fl.oz
50ml	12/3 fl.oz
100ml	31/3 fl.oz
250ml	8 fl.oz
500ml	16 2/3 fl.oz
600ml	20 fl.oz (1pint)
1 litre	13/4 pints

SOLID WEIGHT CONVERSIONS

Metric	Imperial
5g	1/6 oz
10g	1/3 oz
15g	1/2 oz
30g	1 oz
50g	12/3 oz
60g	2 oz
90g	3 oz
100g	31/3 oz
250g	81/3 oz
500g	162/3 oz

OVEN TEMPERATURE CONVERSIONS

°C	Gas	°F
110	1/4	225
120	1/2	250
140	1	275
150	2	300
160	3	325
175	4	350
190	5	375
200	6	400
220	7	425
230	8	450
240	9	475
260	10	500

All weights, measures and servings are approximate conversions.